The Power of
CHOICE

Six Steps to Get What You
Want out of Life

Denise Yosafat

With John Chancellor

The Power of CHOICE is a work of nonfiction. However, some names and personal details have been changed to protect privacy and disguise identities.

Published in the United States by Lavant Publishing

Ordering Information:

Special discounts are available on quantity purchases of ≥ 25 copies for educational use, corporations, associations, and others.

For bulk orders, consulting, coaching, speaking engagements, or copyright reproduction permission requests, please contact Denise Yosafat directly via email at denise@choiceexecutivesolutions.com.

Power of Choice / Denise Yosafat with John Chancellor. —1st ed.

Library of Congress Control Number: 2016910627

Paperback ISBN: 978-0-9976484-0-9
E-book ISBN: 978-0-9976484-1-6

This is dedicated to my wonderfully supportive and loving husband, Wally, and to my inspirational children, Jake, Ariella, and Dylan, who have all made daring, thoughtful and savvy choices in their own lives.

Table of Contents

Introduction

I have vivid dreams. One day I dreamt I was flying overhead and saw tennis shoes tied to a wire. I could tell you in detail what the shoelaces looked like. In another dream I was chasing my son down the highway telling him to go the other way. His Mazda was the same blue as in real life, and I could read his license plate. Another dream had me hosting a party with a bunch of people I never met, but I could tell you what each of them looked like. I am the type who wakes up from dreams sometimes and says, "Did that just happen?"

So it was not a surprise that given all the facilitating I have done in my career, I had a dream where I was writing on a flipchart. Literally, in my dream, I wrote out the word "CHOICE" and all the things that made a "choice" really a "choice." How do we go from ideation to follow-through in all the choices we have in our lives? It was all in my dream. When I woke up, I was energized and excited about it. I felt my dream gave me a true "aha" moment.

At the time, I was working as a master coach training people for their certification, and I mentioned the idea in the dream to one of my fellow master coaches, John Chancellor. He loved the idea and said, "You have to write this. It will help so many people." Followed quickly by, "Can I help?" I said, "Of course. I'd love that." And so it began.

I am a huge believer in the power to shape our own destinies. I researched what causes some people to "stay stuck" and others to make great strides. I looked at how some people deal positively with challenges while others blame their lack of progress on them. Some people lacked process, some lacked skills, and many lacked confidence. It was amazing to me how many of us fear what lies ahead, and let ourselves get paralyzed because of it. Or we don't want to put in the work to make the change we want, even knowing that in the end, we'd be so much happier that we did. Or others didn't even know where to begin or what change they really wanted.

The Power of CHOICE deals with all these issues, in a systemic and caring fashion. It gives step-by-step guidance on what needs to be done next to move you forward, no matter what kind of change you want to make in life. I'm sure my business background in strategic planning and organizational development helped me think through a choice as a process, and my experience in coaching and personal development helped me think through the psychological games we often play with ourselves, and how to overcome them. The combination is truly powerful. Which is why I named this book *The Power of CHOICE*.

As I have given talks and facilitated discussions about this book, I love the stories that people tell me, and how the concepts of the book have impacted them to make positive shifts. I feel honored and privileged every time I can help someone set and move toward their goals and overcome challenges along the way.

As you read through this book, I hope you will open yourself to discover your own power to change and shape your life.

Wishing you a meaningful, happy, fulfilled and successful life!

Denise

P.S. Before you read this book, please visit:

www.PowerofChoiceBook.com

There you can get a ***free checklist self-assessment*** to see how well you make choices now and.... where you can improve!

PART 1:

Before Making a CHOICE

CHAPTER 1
What is CHOICE?

Bald.

I should be bald by now.

With all the hair pulling I have done over my lifetime as I wrangled with what I wanted and how to make tough choices, it is a miracle I have any strands left on my head. Not to mention any feet left with all the pacing. And then there's the emotional eating bit. Chocolate knows how to call out to me exactly when I'm stressed over what to do. You name it. I've tried to destroy my body in many ways while trying to make decisions about which way to go and how to get there.

A lot of times what I wanted was predicated by a problem I had. For instance, here are just a few worries that have caused me sleepless nights over the years:

- How to escape the poverty of my childhood

- How to advance my career when I felt "stuck"

- What to do about some social issues my kids were having

- How to deal with health problems

- How to help my friend going through a tough divorce

- What to do to settle a fight with my husband

- And so on...

And sometimes what I wanted out of life wasn't necessarily caused by a problem, but rather an opportunity to pursue. Like which college should I attend? Or whether to take a higher paying job in another city, even though it meant moving away from family and friends. Or even where to invest some hard earned money...once I had enough to invest.

Life is made up of defining what we want, and figuring out how to get it. It can often be tricky, but it comes down to making *choices* on how to move forward. We are essentially trying to determine and predict what solution will work out best for us. We make a choice to do this versus that or that or that.

It is actually almost impossible to list all the choices we need to make throughout our lives. We have a lot of little choices we make – fairly easy ones, like what to have for dinner - but we also have a lot of big, important, life changing ones. These choices not only have a great impact on our lives, but often the lives of others dear to us. These are the ones that often make us wrangle and doubt ourselves. The ones that make us question our resolve and our decisions.

Why is decision making so darn tough? The answer is that we don't typically think of it as a process. We get so wrapped up in the emotions of it, that we forget there are logical steps we can take to figure out what to do. That is why it is so difficult to make a decision when emotions run high. We just can't think straight. And even when our emotions are in check, and we can think more logically, we still worry about making the wrong decision. We worry that what we are doing will not get us what we want.

But there is an easier way that I've discovered to make a choice. One that is saving me from beating up my body every time a challenge or opportunity comes along. And one that can help you make better choices to get what you want out of life as well.

What I've realized is that to make a choice, you simply need to make a CHOICE.

Let me explain. I realized recently in one of those "aha" hit your forehead with your palm moments that there are six key parts of making any choice, and they just so happen to spell out the word CHOICE. *How convenient is that?*

This book is all about how to use the **Power of CHOICE** by knowing each of its six components and stepping through them one by one. When we do this, we can be more focused on what we want out of life and on how to get it. We can feel more assured that we have thought through and weighed our options. And most importantly, **we can feel more confident that what we are doing is the best decision for us at that point in our lives.** And that, indeed, is powerful.

We will go into each of these steps in detail in the chapters ahead, but for now, let me quickly list them:

(C) Conscious of the problem you want to solve or change you want to make, and WHY

(H) Hopeful of what you want to achieve

(O) Open to different ways to do it

(I) Informed about the different possibilities

(C) Conclusive of what possibility to pursue

(E) Executed into action, tracked, and adjusted as needed

No matter what choice we have, we need to think through each of these steps carefully. Sometimes we can zip through them quickly. Other times, when the decision is harder and has bigger consequences, it takes longer. But if we step through each choice using these six steps, we can ensure our choice was made deliberately and sensibly. We often chastise ourselves for making bad choices, but the more we use this process, the more we improve our chances of making choices that will move us in the direction we want to go.

Let's look at a quick example just to show you how these six steps work. Let's say you know Christmas is a month away.

One simple example of what you want out of life is to make your nephew happy! So now…

C = Conscious

You are **conscious** of the fact that it's time to buy gifts. And that your 12-year old nephew is very dear to you and you'd like to show him how much you care. You're just not sure what to get him.

H = Hopeful

You are **hopeful** that you can make him happy by getting him a special gift. You think ahead to what outcome you want: "My nephew loves the present I got him."

O = Open

You think of different plausible gifts. A kitten? Some books? A CD set? A video game? Some sort of sporting equipment? Maybe a new mitt since last you heard, he was playing baseball. You are **open** to different possibilities.

I = Informed

You ask his mom what interests him right now and what he might want. His mom tells you that he just dropped off his baseball team because the coach wasn't playing him enough. And that he likes Lego sets. You talk to your nephew and casually ask him what's going on in his life as well. Your nephew talks about how cute his friend's new puppy is and how he'd love to have one of his own. And that he just finished reading the *Harry Potter* series of books. He also raves about the high score he just got in a video game.

You also do some browsing online to see the cost of different options so you know which ones might match your budget. By talking to folks and your online research, you become more **informed** about the possible gift ideas.

C = Conclusive

You use this information to start narrowing your choices. Obviously, if he dropped out of baseball, a new mitt wouldn't be appropriate.

You also start thinking of what consequences might happen. Sure, it sounds like your nephew would love a new puppy since he likes his friend's so much, but if you get him one, would he actually take care of it? Will his parents be supportive of a new pet in the house? Likewise, although he likes video games, if you buy a popular, but violent one, will his parents be upset?

After gathering information, and then thinking through likely consequences, and weighing pros and cons, you are **conclusive** that it's best to "play it safe" and buy a Harry Potter Lego Set. You know he likes Legos and likes Harry Potter, and it is non-violent and doesn't require feeding and walking. Plus, you have a coupon that brings it within your budget.

E = Executed

You go out and purchase it. And wrap it up and give it. You **executed** your "safe" gift idea into action! And your nephew gives you a great big thank you hug for it.

Again, this is just a quick example that illustrates the steps. But it shows how each and every step is critical to the process. From being conscious of what you want and are trying to achieve to actually executing the decision. Each step is key and not to be skipped. As we go through this book, we'll cover each of these steps in more detail.

But before we do, let's talk a bit more about choices in general. Because in order to use the six steps of CHOICE most effectively to get what you want out of life, there are two prerequisites:

You believe that you have the power to make choices

AND

You know about the different types of choices in life

Let's examine these both in the next chapters.

CHAPTER 2
The Power to Make Choices

I had a coaching client once who asked me if I could just wave a wand and get him the results he wanted. Alas, I have no such magical powers. But it got me to thinking – wouldn't it be great to have one? Or to even have a genie? You rub a lamp, demand any wish, and the genie makes it happen. Poof! Voila! And you know – to be perfectly honest – if we were limited to three wishes, many of us would use our last wish to ask for more wishes.

Let's face it – life would be so much easier if we could just let others make our dreams come true. We wouldn't have to stress about how to make it happen. But alas, no such genie or magic wand exists. We need to be the ones to figure out not only what we want, but also exactly how we are going to get it.

But often times, we don't.

Case in point: Maggie was living in a marriage of boredom. She complained all the time that her husband wasn't as romantic as he used to be and that he was consumed by work. She felt neglected and constantly told her husband, family and friends how unhappy she was.

But she didn't do anything BUT complain. She started to sound like a broken record. And nothing changed. Why would Maggie go on living in such a situation?

Well, there could be many reasons. One reason is she actually may like the attention and sympathy from others. Or perhaps in her current situation, she can feel superior to her husband – that she's the more involved spouse. We often stay stuck because of a hidden payoff. Maggie may be getting a payoff that is keeping her from doing anything about her current situation.

Or it could be that she truly feels she really has no power to change her circumstance, or even her attitude about it. We say and believe we have no choice in the matter, but the truth is, we always have a choice.

Maggie could leave her husband. Extreme, but it's an option. Or she could sit down with him and ask how they can both relight their spark. She could start being more romantic to see if he will reciprocate. She could take up new hobbies to be less bored, perhaps even something they could do together. There are lots of different options she could consider, but first, she needs to adopt the attitude that she DOES have the power to shape her future. She DOES have the power to get the life she wants.

Choices take work. They take planning, considering, doing. The genie is not here to do it for us – we have to work to get something we want. Have you found yourself ever feeling numb from needing to make a choice? Like you would rather curl up in a ball rather than make it? It sounds baby-like, and it is, but it is also very human. We sometimes feel so overwhelmed by making choices that we just give up the power to do so. Easier to sit back and do nothing than make the wrong choice. Easier to put it on someone else's shoulders or find excuses. Easier to wait and wait and wait until "something" changes versus make the change.

It takes guts to make a change. Guts to make a choice. And we often don't have it. But without it, we often do not get what we want.

If you feel that you are powerless to make a choice and shape your life, well, guess what? You will be powerless to make a choice and shape your life.

One of the worst ways we give up our power to choose is to take on a "victim mentality." This is a learned personality trait that makes us feel like a victim of our circumstances or the negative actions of others. We feel helpless because "they" are doing something to us. Or someone has mistreated us. If you think about it, Maggie had a victim mentality. She felt like the victim to her husband's behavior.

It is a slippery slope with a victim mentality. We might even start to be paranoid that life is out to get us. We talk about how much has gone wrong in our lives versus examining our choices to see what we have done to contribute to our current circumstances. When we feel like a victim, we often feel vengeful, angry, sad and/or hurt. And we feel disempowered.

There are real occasions where we are victims of crimes or when others mistreat us or circumstances are not in our favor. Unfortunately, bad and sometimes awful things *do* happen to good people. And all of us in life have experienced some bad things happening to us – in family, work, health, career, or other areas. But the "victim mentality" keeps us locked in a feeling of helplessness to deal with it. And it even makes us feel righteous that we shouldn't *have* to do anything about it since it's not our fault. But by doing nothing, we continue to feel rage or sorrow. And our self-esteem suffers.

Here's another example: Bill thought his boss was horrible. He said to himself, "I hate this guy. He never gives me the credit I deserve. He seems dismissive when I ask him the simplest question – like he doesn't have time for me or thinks I'm stupid. I feel stuck reporting to this (bleeping) guy." Alas, he felt like the victim at his job.

The good news is that since "victim mentality" is a learned personality trait, it can be unlearned. Or rather, replaced with new learning. Here's an overview of seven key ways we can get out of it and get our power back:

1. Be grateful for what you do have versus resenting what you don't have. Gratitude is huge in helping us start thinking more positively and empowered about life in general. It makes us more confident to take on the day and new challenges.

2. Be forgiving of others who may have wronged you. It is actually a greater benefit to you than the person you forgive. Forgiving allows us to emotionally unlink from the other person, which gives us the ability and clarity to move forward with our own lives. Holding onto grudges just hurts us, not the person who wronged us.

3. Be forgiving of yourself if you feel you put yourself in a bad situation. We all make mistakes, and we will all make more mistakes. Sometimes we feel like the victim of our own actions, and we continue to berate and blame ourselves. Risk taking, experimentation, getting outside our comfort zone, taking a chance – these are all part of life. Accept yourself and past decisions you made – even if they didn't lead to what you wanted.

4. Help someone out. One of the biggest ways we can stop feeling disempowered is to see that we have the power to help others. Not just focusing on what we want out of life, but helping others to get what they want out of life.

5. Likewise, ask for help. There is no shame to say, "I can't do it alone." None of us can do everything by ourselves. Reach out.

6. Take baby steps to move forward. For instance, in the "horrible boss" scenario, maybe Bill can give his boss

a pack of his favorite chewing gum as a small step to build the relationship. When we focus on what we can do, versus what we can't do, our power grows.

7. Plan and organize. When we are disorderly, we feel life is in chaos. The more we can plan, the more control we feel. And the more we can add structure to our lives, the more in control we are. Control helps us feel more powerful.

As you start feeling and doing ANY of these things, you will begin to reshape your victim mentality into one of feeling more empowered to make choices in your life and create the future you want. Resiliency is the power to bounce back from negative circumstances. Instead of locking into victim mode, we bounce back and move on with our lives and make new choices. Our ability to control our destiny is often dependent on how resilient we are.

This "being in control of our destiny" is often difficult for us to accept, but is so critical to making good choices. In fact, my whole way of thinking about it has evolved over the years. I used to tell people that we have two lives: the one in which we are born, and the one we choose to create after childhood. That is because we don't get to pick our genes, and in most cases, we don't get to choose the family or guardians that raise us. But beyond that, it's wide open in what we can choose and how we can shape our destiny. For instance, we can choose to overcome or adjust to physical traits we inherited that may impair us. Or we can choose to complain about them all the time. We can choose to be *like* a loving parent that raised us, or we can choose to be a good, kind, and decent person *instead of* like an abusive parent that raised us. We can choose to take steps to better our lives, or we can choose to stagnate.

I say I USED to tell people we have two lives, and I still do. But now, I think of this differently. Instead of our childhood life, and our adult life, I think of our two lives as being the life in our past, and the life we create in our future, from THIS day forward. To me, this is even more freeing. Starting today, we can choose differently. We can choose a different career, a better relationship, another place to live, or new healthy behaviors. We can choose a positive spiral or a negative one. We can decide to roll with the punches or ball up and cry. We can choose to persist or we can choose to give up. We can choose to inspire or we can choose to hurt. Unless we are impaired with a mental illness that takes away our power to choose, we are born with the ability to make these choices. It's what makes us human. Starting today, we can choose to exercise our humanity – our ability to make choices - even more. And starting today, we can use the Power of CHOICE to help us choose even better, and get more of what we want out of life.

Feeling empowered to make a choice is key when going through the steps of CHOICE. Because *every step of the way, we can have setbacks*, and yet we need to have the courage and persistence to move forward. To focus on what we want to change. To be hopeful about it. To open our minds to possibilities. To gather relevant information. To come to a conclusion. And finally, the courage and persistence to execute on our intentions.

To use the Power of CHOICE most effectively, an absolute prerequisite is to feel you CAN make a choice. No matter what life circumstances you are currently experiencing. If you feel that you CAN make a choice, and that you CAN change your life for the better, and that you CAN seek new opportunities and move toward them, then this six step process will help you do so.

CHAPTER 3
Types of Choices

Once you feel empowered to make choices, then it is a matter of thinking through what kinds of choices there are to make. Often the change we want to make in life, the problem we want to address or opportunity we want to pursue, is staring us right in the face. In this case, we are already in step one – "Conscious" about it. But sometimes we need to think through where we really want to make improvements in our lives. We need to decide what we really want. So let's talk about some of the key types of choices we have.

Life Wheel Choices

LIFE IS ABOUT CHOOSING WHAT BALANCE WORKS BEST FOR US, NOT ABOUT HAVING IT ALL.

Imagine I give you one ball to juggle. Well, that's not so bad – you really just toss it up and down. Okay, two balls now. A little trickier, right? But maybe you can catch one ball while the other's in the air. Okay, now three balls. Whoa! This is getting tough. Balls are dropping. Four balls? Five balls, six balls? You must be out of your mind - at that point, you're hoping they all don't fall down on your head.

Just like juggling balls, we often have trouble "fitting it all in" in life. We do not have time to exercise or we work too much or we can't figure out a way to be highly successful in all areas of our lives. We feel sometimes like we are failing ourselves or disappointing others if we are not pumping on all ten cylinders all the time and accomplishing in all areas of our life. We feel like if we drop any balls, we lose. But guess what? Juggling all the balls at once is rarely doable. At any point in life's journey, we often need to focus on a few areas of life more than others. And these often change as we go through the years – our focus becomes different as our needs, desires, and situations vary. The secret to happiness in life is not in trying to do it ALL, all at once, but in choosing the few key areas to focus on at any given time. It's in prioritizing and reprioritizing as needed. We need to adjust our expectations to match what we choose to focus on versus thinking we can make progress in all areas at once.

The areas of our life can be captured in a pie wheel. But don't be led astray by the perfectly balanced picture – the pie portions are rarely equal. For most of us, a few of these components have a bigger portion of the pie than others, but they are all still there.

Life Wheel

- Career
- Fun, Hobbies, Recreation
- Romance
- Friends
- Family
- Money
- Health
- Locale
- Personal Development
- Spiritual

The life wheel can be used to help you be more conscious of what you might want to focus on to change in your life. Maybe you want to make one slice of the pie bigger. Maybe you want to target on improvements within one or more slices of it. But for now, let's just reflect that all of these ten components are part of your life. In fact, where you are right now in life is based on a number of choices in these areas that you made in the past to shape your current circumstances. So if you are dissatisfied with any of these areas, it often means you are dissatisfied with the choices you made in them. This book is to help you make better choices in the area or areas you most want to improve, so you can get the most out of your life.

Choices in How to Feel

WHEN WE CAN LAUGH AT OURSELVES
AND SMILE THROUGH OUR TEARS,
WE CHOOSE TO MAKE LIFE A HAPPIER PLACE.

We all have good days and bad. We even have great days and awful ones. Days that everything goes well, and days that, well, let's face it, SH*T happens. Grueling day at work (or laid off), fight with our spouse (or a request for divorce), bad cold (or a heart attack), a knee sprain from softball (or a knee blown off in combat), a child not doing well in school (or a child hooked on drugs), a morning where we can't find our car keys (or a day where they were stolen along with the car) - there's a lot of bad that can and does happen in our lives. Some bad we can predict and affect, some we cannot.

The bigger the problem, the harder it is to cope with it. Yet, we CAN choose to feel positive, even when life doesn't go as planned. Not Pollyanna Positive, saying, "All is right with the world all the time." But rather Realistic Positive, saying, "I've got this. I can handle this. I'm not going to let this define me. I am going to pull up my bootstraps and deal with it. I'm going to catch my breath, and decide how to move on. I'm going to choose to adjust, adapt, and take action. I'm going to FEEL capable enough to handle it or FEEL I can get help to do so." Hard? Yes. Really, really hard sometimes? Yes. Worth choosing to feel and do anyway? Undeniably yes.

Let me tell you a story about how I hate bugs. Not phobia hate, but I feel a bit freaked when they crawl around me. When I got my first job out of college, with no money to my name and massive student loan debt, I moved into an ultra-cheap place so I could start saving a little and pay back my loans. With that cheap place came cockroaches. At first I was horrified. I panicked. I jumped every time I turned on the light. But then one day I said to myself, "You chose this place for a reason. Now live with it." So I asked the apartment complex to send an exterminator. That helped for about a week. I asked again. Another week. These suckers were obviously there to stay. So I decided to change the way I FELT about it. I decided instead of feeling grossed out, I'd make friends with them. So, I started naming them and talking to them. "Hi Albert, how are you this morning?" It was a bit unpleasant still (hygiene issues and all), but I chose to feel it was doable. I chose to make light of it. I chose to feel happy about taking steps to become debt free. I chose to feel appreciative of the other aspects of the apartment (like the fact that it was close to work and had a decent shower). And at the end of the lease, I felt proud that I persisted - right before choosing to move into another place that was just a little more expensive but cockroach free!

What bugs you in life, and how can you choose to feel differently about it?

Here's another more serious example. One of the students at the coaching academy where I worked has Stage 4 colon cancer. The survival rate statistic is less than thirty percent. She is a single mother with a young child. She went in for a colonoscopy because she was having issues, and was hospitalized immediately with the diagnosis. She was shocked, to say the least. Yet, she chose not to let despair rule her. In fact, she not only chose to fight her horrible diagnosis, but she chose to use her predicament as a platform to go out and make sure others get routine check-ups that could save their lives. She posted messages of hope and messages of care on YouTube, Facebook, and on her own website. She held parties at the hospital for other patients going through similar treatment to help lift their spirits. She posted all the horrible physical side effects of chemo and medication and invasive procedures she was experiencing, but always ended with chipper messages showing she was still fighting the fight, and wanted to help others avoid the fight altogether with early diagnosis. She chose to FEEL empowered, to be strong, a fighter, an educator, a motivator, a doer, an angel, and an overall inspiration to others. With life hitting her hard in the face, she chose to not only retain her caring and thoughtful spirit, but to shine it on the world.

How many of us would have felt defeated, depressed, devastated, destabilized, debilitated, and a million other demonic thoughts? I am not saying she does not have days where she feels extreme sadness and excruciating pain – how could you not with such a challenge? I am not saying she doesn't worry about the current and future welfare of her child and other loved ones. She does. But she chose to rise above the physical fray and let her mind focus on the positive she could generate from her situation. She chose to be a positive light to others versus curse out the world for doing this to her.

A lot of times we choose not to feel positive because we let the negative voice in our head win. There are days when we feel better about ourselves, and days when we berate ourselves. Sometimes we belittle ourselves because we believe what others have said about us – we let them judge us and we start to believe the negative that they spew about us. Sometimes we compare ourselves to others, and just feel we don't measure up. Or we chastise ourselves because we failed at something. We feel weak, stupid, unworthy, or a multitude of other negative emotions. And we can easily let ourselves spiral down.

But even in our darkest moments, we CAN choose to be nicer to ourselves. We can choose to stop badmouthing ourselves. We can choose to learn from our failures and mistakes versus kick ourselves because of them. We can choose to pat ourselves on the back and say, "Hey, good job for trying! Way to take a risk." We can choose to view life as an adventure full of lab experiments – some work, some don't – and give ourselves a break for those that don't work. We can realize that if you're not making any mistakes or failing, you are probably choosing to play it too safe, not stretch yourself far enough, not grow. Accidents happen, failures happen, mistakes happen. We can choose to FEEL more positively about any of them.

Below is a chart that you can use to think about positive and negative feelings that you can choose to have at any given time:

JOYFUL	PEACEFUL	CONFIDENT	SAD	UPSET	FRIGHTENED
Energized	Content	Strong	Inadequate	Hostile	Insecure
Fascinated	Thoughtful	Respected	Ashamed	Hateful	Anxious
Stimulated	Responsive	Worthwhile	Depressed	Frustrated	Helpless
Playful	Relaxed	Important	Miserable	Selfish	Rejected
Sexy	Sentimental	Appreciated	Inferior	Jealous	Submissive
Creative	Grateful	Satisfied	Unworthy	Hurtful	Foolish
Aware	Loving	Intelligent	Guilty	Critical	Discouraged
Excited	Nurturing	Certain	Stupid	Infuriated	Confused
Daring	Trusting	Hopeful	Lonely	Angry	Insignificant
Delighted	Intimate	Determined	Bored	Enraged	Scared
Amused	Calm	Established	Apathetic	Righteous	Weak
Willing	Reflective	Persistent	Fatigued	Judgmental	Oppressed

The more we choose positive feelings, the healthier we become emotionally. The more positive we embrace, the more we enjoy life and feel accomplished. We have a higher zest for living and a higher ability to have fun. We have a better way to deal with our stresses and bounce back from adversity. We have a greater flexibility to deal with new situations and to adapt and learn new things. We have a greater sense of purpose and meaning in our lives and in our relationships.

Belief Choices

WHETHER WE DECIDE TO KEEP OUR BELIEFS
OR CHOOSE TO CHANGE THEM,
OUR BELIEFS SHAPE OUR ACTIONS.

When you were little, did you believe in the tooth fairy? If so, did you make sure to put your tooth under your pillow so the tooth fairy would find it and leave you a little money for it?

This is a simple example of how our beliefs shape our actions. We would never have left a tooth under our pillow had we not believed a little fairy was going to come get it and leave us something in return.

We often think about our beliefs only as spiritual or religious in nature – how or if we believe in a higher power. Some believe that Jesus is the son of God while others believe that keeping kosher is in accordance with God's will. Some believe that there is no God but Allah while others believe in the oneness of God and humankind. There are those who believe in the individualized expression of the cosmic source, and those who believe making an offering to a volcano will protect them. Some believe in angels and demons. Some people believe in reincarnation as a path to Nirvana and others believe in an afterlife in Heaven. People believe in the Bible, Koran, Torah, Vedas, or other holy scriptures as the official word of God. Or they believe God doesn't even exist. Some believe there is only one path to eternal life while others believe it can be reached by a life of selfless service and being good and kind. Some believe in hell for those who sinned in life and didn't atone, while others believe only in a white light for all. This is just a sampling of some religious beliefs - there are thousands of them. If you search for "beliefs" on the Internet, it is typically religious ones that come up first, since these are what we most commonly think of when we say the word "belief."

Belief is a state-of-mind in which we regard something – an assumption or conviction - to be true. We as humans can endlessly debate what is really true when it comes to religion. Our beliefs in this area often depend on our upbringing. But then we get to adulthood, and some people choose to change their religious beliefs. They decide to convert to another religion with a new set of beliefs.

These people choose to believe differently.

But religious beliefs are just one kind. As members of society, we also have cultural beliefs. In the United States, we often believe in the benefit of capitalism and individualism versus communism. We may believe in the "American Dream" - that anything is possible if we study and work hard enough. We may believe that different regions have different attitudes – that people in the Midwest are friendlier, in the East Coast more sophisticated, in the South homier, and in the West more free-spirited. We may even believe in our cultural norms, like the American norm that women's armpits and legs need to be shaved to be acceptable. A lot of beliefs are based on cultural norms like this.

We can choose to agree with these cultural beliefs, or we can choose to believe that all or some of them are untrue or at least unnecessary. Some women throw away the razor and say, "Accept me as I am!"

Some beliefs are innocuous, while others, like prejudices, are damaging. In many cases, prejudices are based on stereotypes, which are simplified assumptions about a group often not based in reason or experience. But we use any experience we can to strengthen them. We might generalize to believe ALL people of a certain race, religion, culture, gender, age, or sexual orientation are a certain way.

I knew a man named Sam who was very prejudiced against black people. The prejudice started when his parents told him they were inferior. Then he was robbed once, and the person happened to be black. He was bumped on a subway, and the person who did it and did not apologize was black. He heard a news story of a man beating his wife, and he happened to be black. He consciously and unconsciously built up "evidence" that what his parents told him really was true. He believed it to be so.

Of course, he ignored other evidence that countered this. He probably ignored a nice saleslady who happened to be black. Or he ignored the generosity and astuteness of a black entrepreneur that was in the news. Or he looked at Oprah as a fluke – not the norm – because he thought "blacks aren't like that." And he ignored the fact that people of other colors committed crimes, acted rude, and misbehaved in a number of other different ways. When we have a belief, we tend to look for evidence to support it, and ignore evidence that disproves it. Prejudices, like other beliefs, are supported by evidence we choose to enforce them.

But once we recognize that we have a prejudicial belief, we can choose to change it. We can choose to question our assumptions, look for examples that disprove our belief, and recognize the folly in our thinking.

We talked earlier about negative feelings we can have about ourselves. We often have negative beliefs about ourselves as well. Remember, a belief is a state of mind, in which we regard something – an assumption or conviction - to be true. So, if we believe we are too shy to speak in public, this "truth" will keep us from getting up and speaking. If we believe we are not worthy of a good relationship where we feel loved and supported, we settle for one that is bad and abusive. If we believe we are not a good writer, we don't venture to write a book. If we believe we can't do well in school, we stop trying. If we believe we'll be rejected if we ask a person to go on a date, we don't even approach someone to whom we are attracted.

Our beliefs about ourselves can start anytime. Someone might plant a thought into our head, and then we look for supportive evidence to prove that it's true, and the belief grows and grows. If this is a negative thought, then it grows like a weed. If it is a positive one, it blossoms like a flower. Or we may have a bad experience and we begin to believe badly about ourselves because of it. Just like we stereotype others, "Irish people are always like this, homosexuals are always like that," we do the same damage to ourselves. "I'm always like this or that." "I can never do this or that." "I am not capable enough for this or that."

What beliefs do you have about yourself or others, and which do you want to change?

Behavior Choices

IT IS HOW WE CHOOSE TO BEHAVE
THAT HAS THE GREATEST IMPACT ON OTHERS,
AND ON OUR OWN SUCCESS IN LIFE.

Trying to understand why some people behave as they do is like trying to jump up to the moon. We can never know what is inside another person's head (at least not with today's technology – still waiting on the Vulcan mind meld), and so we don't know what drives them to act the way they do. We can make educated guesses, but often by doing so we make incorrect assumptions. But the good news is that while we might not understand someone else's behavior, we can make an effort to comprehend and *make choices* about our own. We can try to understand better why we do the things we do, and we can certainly decide we want to change certain behaviors that are counterproductive, hurtful, or just out and out bad.

There are many, many influences on our behavior at any given time. Our beliefs, our feelings, our personality type, our environment, the people around us, the circumstances we're encountering, our level of stress, and our past experiences all play a part.

We talked a bit already about how our beliefs and feelings affect behavior. But they affect them in different ways. One person may feel angry and they scream and yell. Another person may feel angry and they hold it in and give the silent treatment. Yet another may feel angry and decide to write down their feelings to cope with them. Or another might want to quietly discuss the reason for their anger and see if there is a solution to alleviate it.

This is an example of how different personality types can affect behavior. We have introverts and extroverts, people who are more organized and precise and those who are more flexible and open-minded, folks who are more sensitive and empathetic and others who are more logical and pragmatic, people who are more intuitive and idealistic, and those who need to learn through experience and are more realistic. Lots and lots of differences that can impact how we behave in any given situation.

Our environment and the people around us also can affect our behavior. We all behave at least somewhat differently in front of different people – for instance, being more professional in a work environment and more relaxed in a social one. Can you imagine if a twenty-something with an active social life took his party hardy behavior to work? He'd be fired in a heartbeat. Sometimes these behavior differences go to extremes. I have met abusive husbands who are charming and kind when around others. No one suspects this is the same person who tells his wife she's worthless and that she sickens him - how can he behave so meanly to her when he's so nice in public? We meet kids who are respectful one-on-one, but become bullies to impress their friends. Who we are around – our environment as well as the people involved – can affect our behavior.

Our circumstances, and often the level of stress they bring, can impact our behavior as well. If we find ourselves unexpectedly laid off or have another set back, we may behave differently than when "all is right with the world." I remember well when my father went from riches to rags and then, as he struggled financially, had kidney failure – this man with such a jolly personality didn't tell jokes much anymore nor did he smile as much. He let his circumstances influence his good-natured behavior.

Our past often influences our behavior as well. We may stop trying new things if we took a risk and experienced failure. We may model our parents' behavior because that is what we know, even if that behavior is bad. We may turn to a crutch of drugs, alcohol or overeating to try to escape the emotions tied to the past.

With all these strong influences on our behavior, can we really choose to change it? The answer is a resounding yes. Behavior modification can and does happen all the time. We CAN choose to behave differently. Sometimes this just takes the will to decide to do things differently, and sometimes it takes learning new skills.

For instance, you can decide one day to just be nicer to your husband. You can decide to start kissing him good morning and good night, stop pointing out his faults, give him a shoulder rub, ask him about his day, and listen. This doesn't necessarily take any new training or skill – just the determination and willingness to begin to act differently. Other behavior modifications DO take new learning and personal development. If you are locked in he said/she said arguments all the time, you may need to learn to communicate and negotiate more effectively. The first part is choosing to improve in this area, and the second part is learning how to do so.

The other key part to behavior modification is reward. Whenever we have intrinsic, internal rewards for choosing to change a behavior and then actually changing it, the more successful that behavior modification will be. Buying a new car to reward yourself for losing weight might be great as a temporary reward, but eventually that new car will become old and your old behavior more likely to return. A more permanent reward is the feeling of pride and comfort when you look in the mirror and think, "I did it! I'm strong. I'm capable." And then give yourself a hug and pat on the back. The feeling of euphoria from an accomplishment will last a lot longer than a material reward, and will make you want to hang onto that feeling more by staying with the behavior modification longer (or hopefully forever).

Much like positive and negative feelings, we can list positive and negative behaviors. On the following pages are some examples of behaviors that are positive and negative.

POSITIVE BEHAVIORS:

Help others	Respect others	Be open to possibilities
Smile	Appreciate	Give credit where due
Encourage	Act responsibly	Play
Be faithful	Show empathy	Calmly discuss
Make others laugh	Be considerate	Nurture
Exhibit good manners	Play fair	Be friendly
Tell the truth	Apologize when you hurt someone	Follow through on commitments
Exercise	Tolerate differences	Relax
Share	Love	Communicate effectively
Be thoughtful	Show enthusiasm	Compromise
Practice moderation	Adapt	Be collaborative
Act forgiving	Be careful	Produce
Be assertive	Influence positively	Plan carefully
Compliment	Hug	Learn

NEGATIVE BEHAVIORS:

Hurt others	Disrespect others	Be closed to possibilities
Frown	Be ungrateful	Hog credit
Discourage	Act irresponsibly	Be sullen
Cheat on a loved one	Show indifference	Yell and scream
Make others irate	Be inconsiderate	Neglect
Be rude	Play dirty	Be unfriendly
Lie	Be unapologetic	Ignore commitments
Be slovenly	Be judgmental	Stress out
Be selfish	Hate	Communicate ineffectively
Act uncaring	Show apathy	Confront
Overindulge	Stagnate	Be domineering
Seek revenge	Act recklessly	Destroy
Be aggressive	Be manipulative	Be careless
Criticize	Hit	Act ignorantly

Take a look at these lists. Are there any behaviors that you recognize in yourself, and that you choose to change?

Now that you feel empowered to make choices, and you realize the types of choices that can be made, let the **Power of CHOICE** begin!

PART 2:

Making a CHOICE

CHAPTER 4

CHOICE

C is for CONSCIOUS

It is important not just to be awake for our choices,
but to be aware of our choices.

Conscious:

1. Fully aware of or sensitive to something

2. Having our mental faculties fully active

3. Known to oneself; felt

4. Aware of what one is doing

5. Aware of oneself

6. Deliberate; intentional

So, not to get confusing, but do you know we make multiple layers of choices even around the simplest choices? WHAT? Okay, let me explain. Say you are watching TV on the couch next to your teenage daughter and you decide you want to snack on some ice cream. You stand up, walk to the freezer, open it, take out the ice cream, and put a couple scoops in a bowl. Then sit back down on the couch to eat it.

Here are some of the choices you make along the way:

1) I choose to eat

2) I choose to eat something sweet

3) I choose ice cream as the something sweet

4) I choose vanilla as the flavor

5) I choose Friendly's as the brand

6) I choose to eat it from a bowl

7) I choose to eat it at home

8) I choose to eat it despite expecting my daughter (little stinker!) to look at me, roll her eyes, and call me a couch potato.

9) I choose to feel guilty about eating something that is not the healthiest for me

10) I choose to believe I have no will power.

Now, we may not THINK of some of these as choices, because we instantly rule out alternatives. For instance, it may not even *consciously* cross our mind to:

1) Not eat anything versus eat

2) Or eat something salty versus sweet

3) Or eat a cookie versus ice cream as the something sweet

4) Or choose strawberry versus vanilla

5) Or choose Edy's as the brand versus Friendly's

6) Or choose a cone versus eating from a bowl

7) Or choose to eat at a Friendly's restaurant versus eating at home

8) Or choose to eat carrots with hummus to role model to our daughter healthy eating habits (and avoid any snarky remarks)

9) Or choose to feel we deserve a treat after a long day at work

10) Or choose to believe that treats are great, as long as they are in moderation and that I am capable of eating them in moderation

Wow! So many choices around one little bowl of ice cream. Now, you might say that not all of these are real choices. For instance, maybe you only had Friendly's vanilla ice cream in your freezer, so another brand or flavor wasn't an alternative at the time. But at some point, someone chose to buy Friendly's vanilla and put it in the freezer. So a choice was still made somewhere along the line.

We make SO many choices every single day that it would boggle our mind to think through every single one and ruminate over it. We just would never have the time. Certain decisions need to be or can be made quickly while more important choices often take more time, and need to be more deliberate and intentional.

In fact, thankfully, some of the decisions that are made very quickly become routines. And those routines, after repetition, become habits. We don't *consciously* make choices about them anymore, because we have built them as regular activities in our lives. We don't wake up and consciously think, "Should I go to the bathroom and do my business in the toilet, or today should I use a chamber pot or maybe a cooking pot since I don't own a chamber pot?" Or, "Today, should I brush my teeth, or go around with plaque and bad breath all day?" We COULD make those choices, and in actuality, we made the choice a long time ago (when potty training, for instance), and have just decided to stick with that choice. So we don't really need to consciously think about it anymore. We form routine habits that make it easier for us to get through the day without having to think about our choices on everything.

Of course, there is the bad side to habits as well. While good habits make it easier for us to get through the day without having to *consciously* decide everything, bad habits, like nail biting or skipping breakfast, mean we unconsciously do things that are not so nice. While we don't consciously choose to do these behaviors anymore once they become habits, we CAN choose to change the habit. Habits are difficult to change, but certainly still changeable. But first it takes a conscious choice to do so.

Let me share an experiment with you about consciously changing habits. Professor Ben Fletcher of the University of Hertfordshire, United Kingdom, conducted a series of psychological experiments. He worked with groups of people and each day he had them pick a different option from contrasting behaviors. He gave them a set of cards, and on one side of each card was a particular behavior. On the other side was the opposite behavior. For example, he had lively/quiet, silly/serious, reactive/proactive, shy/flirty, introvert/extrovert, passive/assertive, generous/stingy, etc. Each morning a person would pick a card from the stack. They would look at the card and decide which behavior was their normal. Then for that day they were supposed to engage in the contrasting behavior as often as possible.

If they were normally shy, they would try to be flirty all day long. If they were normally quiet, they needed to try to be as lively as possible for that day. They were also instructed to take at least one action per day that was outside their comfort zone. So, in addition to acting opposite to their normal routine for a particular behavior, they were instructed to do something that made them uncomfortable.

Now here is what was interesting. After four months, Dr. Fletcher found that the participants had lost an average of eleven pounds. Now the experiment was not about weight loss. That was a by-product. What was interesting is that once the participants started paying attention to their behavior, they became more *conscious* of their choices. They stopped acting like robots and actually took control of their lives. They started making better choices.

Dr. Fletcher calls this "FIT" Science – "Framework for Internal Transformation." It is important that you be open to new ideas. But unless you stop acting out of habit, you will not have the opportunity to make conscious choices to move in the direction you want.

You can try this experiment on your own. Just get a dozen or so index cards. Write down some behaviors like those previously listed. Then on the reverse side of the card, write the opposite behavior. You should have at least a dozen different behaviors. Then each morning, select a card. If the card says shy/flirty, decide what your usual behavior is. Then for that day, do the opposite. Leave that card out of the deck, and the next morning, repeat the process. When the deck is depleted, put all the cards back in the deck and start over. You will be surprised at how conscious you become about the choices you are making.

We can usually, with effort, consciously change our habits. When a habit becomes an addiction however, it becomes even tougher to change. We lose a greater sense of control over what we are doing, taking or using. There are many different studies related to behavioral and substance addictions – posits that they may be classified along a spectrum of impulsive-compulsive disorders, research that looks at the chemistry in our brains that may lead to these addictions and support them, and many different studies on how to best treat them. Addictions are the hardest behaviors to modify; yet many people do choose to change them and go on to live healthier lives. It needs to start with the awareness that the behavior is impeding your wellbeing. This needs to be followed by the willingness to take dramatic steps to change it. That effort may include rehabilitation, weekly support meetings like Alcoholics or Gamblers Anonymous, nicotine patches, or other methods to deal with addictive behaviors. But it all starts with *being aware* that the behavior is causing harm, and a *conscious* choice to change it. Net, while habits take no conscious thought to do, and addictions often take over control of our thoughts, we CAN still make the choice to change them if we want.

The first part about making any choice is moving it into our conscious mind.

We need to become aware of it in order to address it. As part of this, we need to define what choice we really want to make. For instance, let's say you are overweight. You feel sluggish and you are worried about being a bad role model to your kids. You look in the mirror and see only fat rolls. You feel that food is controlling you versus you controlling your food. Your negative body image has impacted your self-image, and you constantly are criticizing yourself. And then one day you say, "Enough!" You decide you want to make a change. You **consciously** decide you want something different in life.

But, do you really? Because now we need to examine the strength of your "why." If you do not have a strong enough "why," you will never make it a priority to change.

Og Mandino once said, "Failure will never overtake me if my determination to succeed is strong enough." In other words, if your "why" is strong enough, you will be able to succeed at any reasonable undertaking. You will work to overcome obstacles along the way, even if and when they seem insurmountable.

So what do we mean about your "Why?" It simply means the motivation behind whatever you are attempting to do. Instead of talking abstract, let's work on a concrete example. Suppose you want to start a new consulting business. If you've even thought about starting a business, you know the odds are daunting and there are countless challenges and barriers standing in your way.

Here are some reasons you may give for wanting to start your own consulting business:

1) I want to make lots of money

2) I want to be able to work when and how I want to, on my own terms.

3) I want to prove to people that I am capable

4) I have a real passion to help others find success

5) My son is a special needs child and I think this is the best way I can provide the support he needs. I can earn income and also have much needed flexibility for him.

If you think about these reasons, the "why" goes from external to internal as you move down the list. Making lots of money is usually not a strong motivator. The majority of people profess to want to be a millionaire, but most will not come close to doing the work necessary to achieve that goal. Money is an external versus internal motivator, and external motivators are not as lasting.

But if you have a special needs child and you feel the best way you can adequately provide for that child is to start and grow your own business, you will jump out of bed each and every day ready to face the challenges of running your business. Your child's welfare is at stake, and you will do what's necessary to protect it and provide him the support needed.

So what makes a strong "Why?"

First it needs to be something <u>you</u> want. If you are making choices based on what you think someone else wants, you will never have a strong "why." Feeling like you have control over your own life is one of the strong basic drives of humans. You must feel that the choice is yours.

Second, it needs to be aligned with your values. Short term, we may do things that are not in alignment with our values. Long term, our actions must align with them. So if you are attempting to make choices that do not align with your values, you will find it harder and harder to stick with the choices you are making.

Third, the choices you make that have a greater good component will be much stronger than a choice that only benefits you. In the above example, making a choice for a special needs child provides a much stronger drive than working for a fancy sports car that you can drive around and use to impress people.

If you look at some of the most harmful behaviors – obesity, smoking, drug addiction, compulsive gambling, the primary person who would benefit from better choices around these behaviors is the person engaging in the self-destructive behavior. Therefore, the "Why" is often not strong enough for the person to change their behavior.

If you can get the person engaged in the self-destructive behavior to see another person as the primary beneficiary, it is easier for them to make better choices. For example, some women quit smoking when pregnant. Their baby's healthy development is a stronger motivation for change.

We are often ambivalent around our toughest choices. That is, there are some strong factors pulling us to change and some equally strong factors in favor of maintaining the status quo. Unless we can get clear on some strong reasons why we should change, why we need to make better choices, and ultimately, why we should prioritize the change in our life, the tug of war between change and status quo is likely to keep us stuck.

In his comedy routine, W. C. Fields said, "Now don't say you can't swear off drinking; it's easy. I've done it a thousand times." This is the tug of war between competing behaviors. We want to quit smoking, drinking, unhealthy eating or any number of other behaviors. But we are getting some benefits from the behavior. Meaning, the tugs for us not to change outweigh the change, so we do not prioritize it.

Unless we believe our "why" – the benefits we can gain - are stronger than what we give up, our choice to get what we think we want out of life will not be permanent.

If you are struggling to make a change in behavior or direction, you need to take some time and write out your reason why. Get clear on what is driving the change – is it you, or are you being pressured by a relationship partner, employer, or friend? You may want to write out your values around this behavior. What matters to you? Does what you want out of life align with your values? Will it serve a greater good?

Priority and Ease of Choice

A strong "why" creates a priority to make a change. We feel *compelled* to change. One way to think about this is a sliding scale. **On a scale of 1-10**, what is the priority of a particular choice you need to make? The more significance the choice has on your life and the life of others dear to you, the higher you could rate it. This rating varies by person. For instance, let's take that bowl of ice cream from the beginning of the chapter. For many people, it may have a significance of 1, since it doesn't impact them much. They like ice cream, they eat the ice cream, and it's no big deal. Whether they eat ice cream today or not isn't going to affect them much. There's no big reason *why* they need to give it a second thought.

LEVEL OF PRIORITY: 1

For other people, like the woman who is overweight, the impact may be rated a bit higher because that little bowl of ice cream may lead her to negative feelings of having no control and a downward spiral of beating herself up because of it. So her reasons not to eat it become more significant, and it becomes a bigger priority to avoid the ice cream.

LEVEL OF PRIORITY: 4

Types of choices that have an even greater priority in our life are the ones that impact us the most. These tend to be a lot of the categories on our life wheel – career, relationships, where we live, and other choices that greatly influence how we feel about life.

A scale of 1-10 could also be used to rate feelings, beliefs, and behaviors as well. For instance, how important is it for us to *feel* a sense of belonging in our religion? Why do we need this? How important is it for us to *believe* in tolerance towards others? What are our reasons for wanting this? How important is it for us to *behave* respectfully to our spouse? Again, answer the "why."

Likewise, we can use sliding scales for levels of difficulty. Choosing ice cream as a snack might not be a difficult decision. You like it and it's available in the house, so it's easy to decide.

LEVEL OF DIFFICULTY: 1

But what if you had a craving for ice cream and there is none in the house, and the closest store is five miles away and there's a blizzard outside. Now the inconvenience is an issue that makes getting ice cream much more difficult.

LEVEL OF DIFFICULTY: 5

Of course, we're still talking ice cream. The bigger decisions in life are often much more difficult to make. For instance, choosing what to major in at college, especially if you are not sure, might be this:

LEVEL OF DIFFICULTY: 8

And, again, a level of difficulty can be applied to feelings, beliefs and behaviors. How difficult do we find it to *feel* compassion for someone who hurt us? How difficult is it for us to *believe* in ourselves and in our abilities? How difficult is it to *behave* calmly when an employee just made a big mistake that caused the business to lose a client?

For each of us, the level of priority (the strength of our "why") and the level of difficulty for any decision are very personal. The simplest decision for one person may be the hardest for another. One person may put a high priority on one part of their life, while the other could care less about the same choice. For instance, one person may feel it is a high priority to feel altruistic while another person could care less about being so. One may put a high priority on behaving "political correct," while another puts a high priority on behaving genuine to themselves, whether politically correct or not. Likewise, one person may find it very easy to be respectful, while another person finds it very difficult to talk calmly when angry.

One way to think about priority and ease is to draw out a simple grid, putting the level of priority on the bottom and the level of difficulty on the side. Of course, we would not put ALL our choices on this grid – at least not at once - it would become overcrowded in a heartbeat. But we can use this as a general tool to understand our own priorities and how much difficulty we are having with our choices, and to even redistribute where we are putting our time and effort based on this understanding. So let's take a look at this grid and see how it might help us make choices about where we want to focus in our life.

There are four boxes to the grid – high priority & high difficulty, low priority & low difficulty, high priority and low difficulty, and low priority and high difficulty. Believe it or not, every single choice we make in life fits somewhere in one of those boxes. Sometimes consciously, sometimes subconsciously. This grid can be used as a tool to think about your choices more consciously. So as you look at the grid on the following page, think about a current choice you are considering and where it might fit.

	Low Difficulty	
	High Difficulty	
	Low Priority	High Priority

Let me give an example of how to use this grid. When I was a child and dreamed about getting married one day, the choice of whom to marry was extremely important, because it impacted my life so much. My "why" was strong – I wanted the stability, the lifelong love, the support, the friendship, and all the reasons we often associate with a good marriage. Finding "the right one" was a high priority. When I met my husband, I quickly fell in love with him, as he did with me. It was not a difficult decision for us to know we both wanted to spend a lifetime together. In fact, after two relationships that lasted over a year each, I met him, and decided after only two months of dating that he was the right one for me.

The decision came almost naturally as I quickly checked off the following in my mind:

- He's cute/I'm romantically attracted to him

- He makes me laugh

- He has a good job/good education

- He is the same religion

- He comes from a loving family (who seems to like me – bonus!)

- He plays accordion (okay, this really wasn't part of my checklist, but it was kind of interesting)

- He seems to accept my quirks (like overcooking my spaghetti sauce since I like it pasty)

- He is thoughtful

- He doesn't mind that I don't make my bed all the time (so he's easygoing)

Net, I had a laundry list of reasons for wanting to marry him, and so it became a priority to me to do so. It was very natural to be with him, so the decision to spend the rest of my life with him was easy for me. He must have felt the same way, since we just one day started talking about "when we get married" and how we could save to pay for our wedding. For both of us, the priority to marry each other was high, and the difficulty of the decision rather low.

Over thirty years later, it is still an easy decision to stay together, and a top priority to do so, even when we get into arguments. Dealing with each other's stubbornness, impatience, and tempers has not daunted us from the feeling that it is right to be together.

For us, the choices to get married, and stay married, were high priority and easy. On the following page, we see how these fit on the chart.

Low Difficulty		● Get Married ● Stay Married
High Difficulty		
	Low Priority	High Priority

Notice how "stay married" is a little lower on this chart – because it is more difficult than getting married. Planning for a wedding has challenges, but living out a lifetime together has a lot more challenges. Marriages that are in deep trouble might have "Stay Married" on the bottom half of the chart: it might become a high priority to stay together, but highly difficult to do so. Great effort needs to be taken to repair the marriage in order for it to continue. There are other marriages where one or both partners just get to a point where it is a low priority to stay together. Too much hurt, pain, anger and suffering, and too little will and commitment to improve the marriage, making a divorce highly likely. The "why stay together" just isn't there anymore. If the priority to stay together shifts from high to low, then there is less willingness to go the extra mile (or even two or three or more extra miles) to rejuvenate the marriage.

Notice also how "Stay Married" is to the right of "Get Married." Getting married was a huge priority, but staying married is an even bigger one, especially now that we have a family. It is easier to break apart when there are no kids involved, but the commitment and "why" for us became even stronger once our children were born. It became an even greater priority for us to work through any problems and role model to our kids how to do so.

Let's take another example. Say you want to grow your business by increasing the number of clientele. This is a high priority to you. You have a lot of reasons why you want to grow, but you are not quite sure how to do it. You may need to seek additional training in social media and/or other forms of marketing. You might need to seek out a business mentor. There are a lot of possibilities for what to do, but for you, most of them are daunting. For you, "increasing clientele" is a high priority/high difficulty decision:

	Low Priority	High Priority
Low Difficulty		
High Difficulty		● Increase Clientele

What about choices that are low priority in our lives? Well, we have lots of those. What sweater to buy? What to serve at Thanksgiving? When to phone an old friend? What font to use on a letter? How to decorate our office? Which shoes go with what outfit? Are these really high priority decisions? Do they really matter in the great scheme of things? Will they greatly change the course of our lives? Usually not. As Dr. Richard Carlson alluded to in his book *Don't Sweat the Small Stuff...and it's all Small Stuff*, we often give too much priority to rather insignificant decisions in our lives. We stress and we fret about them. We can take any of these decisions and give them whatever priority we want. But let's be conscious of WHY we are prioritizing them as such, and do they really deserve that degree of priority? Do they deserve the time and attention we are giving them? Do they deserve to make us sweat?

This is especially true for decisions that fall into the bottom left square. They are low priority, yet may take an enormous amount of effort to accomplish them since they are highly difficult. And often, with that effort, come the frustrations, worries, panic, and feelings of unworthiness as we struggle to complete something that...isn't even a priority! Why do we torture ourselves this way? Do we need to do these? The more of these choices we can avoid, the more time we will have to focus on what we really want out of life.

For decisions that are low priority but not that difficult - the "easy peasy" ones – well, we might as well do them, but only *if we have the time*. If we find ourselves filling our lives with low priority decisions – even easy ones - at the expense of high priority ones, we need to consciously reevaluate where we are spending our time. For instance, if we are putting off work on an important project because it is easier to choose a movie to go see, we are not consciously getting our priorities straight. We need to stop and think, "Is this where I want to spend my time right now? Is this going to make me feel better in the long run about moving ahead with this project? Am I going to meet the project deadlines if I do this?" Perhaps you do have time to see the movie and still complete your project on time, or perhaps you don't. The key is to make it a conscious choice so you think through the implications.

Anything that is in the top right hand quadrant of this chart – the high priority decisions that are easy to do is what we call "low hanging fruit." If they are high priority, and we can easily do them, then might as well "pick" them to do. These are no brainers to pursue. They are meaningful, yet easy. They can make a huge difference in your life and yet do not take a lot of effort. A total win-win. There may not be a lot of these in our lives, but when they come along, grab them. For instance, it may be a high priority decision of where to live and raise your family, and it may be an easy decision because the job you want is right near extended family so you already have a sense of belonging and support. Makes the decision easy.

So what does all this mean when it comes to being conscious of the choices we are making in life? Well, if we look back to the chart, it comes down to this:

> Say YES to those things in life that are high priority and are easy to do, feel or believe. When our "Why" is strong, and it is easy to do, these should always be pursued.

> Say PROBABLY to those things in life that are high priority, but take effort – they tend to be well worth it in the end. This could be changing part of your life wheel (relationship, job…) or even changing a negative behavior, feeling, or belief. It may take effort, but you will feel a strong emotional benefit and a sense of accomplishment as you take steps to change.

> Say MAYBE to those things in life that are not high priority, but are also not hard to do. Fit these in when you have time, but not in place of high priority choices. Likewise, with beliefs, feelings or behaviors that don't impact your life that much. No need to focus on these or worry about changing them, but you can if you have time.

> Say NO as much as possible to those things in life that you do not prioritize and that take too much effort – these only cause needless stress and frustration.

	Low Priority	High Priority
Low Difficulty	MAYBE	YES!!!!!
High Difficulty	NO	PROBABLY

It is often helpful to use this chart as a visual tool to examine a potential change you want to make. Where does it fit in the quadrants? Do your reasons "why" make it a high priority? Is it worth the difficulty of doing it? Is this change something you really want out of life?

Being Conscious of our Subconscious

When we make choices, we aren't always even aware of WHY we are making those choices. We often don't sit and think about what is causing us to act the way we do. We don't often say, "Why am I sitting down and eating a bowl of chips? Why am I stressing at the thought of taking a test? Why am I avoiding this sales call? Why am I staying in a relationship despite being abused? Why am I being a wallflower at this party? Why am I obsessive about cleaning? Why am I yelling at my kid right now versus discussing an issue with them calmly? Why?"

We often don't know the answer to our "why?" question...and often don't even bother to ask the question. We don't analyze why we feel a certain way or act a certain way. Instead, we often do things based on what our subconscious minds dictate.

Let's talk a little about conscious versus subconscious. One easy way to think about it is in terms of a new experience, like driving. When you first start to drive, you are aware of everything you need to do as you drive the car. You focus on the road, you think about your turn signals, you check and recheck mirrors – it takes effort since it is so new to you. Your choices are made at a very conscious level since you have to think about them. But as you get more experienced, your driving skills improve and your actions and reactions go on autopilot. You don't think, "Do I need to click my turn signal on now?" You just do it. Your skills have been implanted in your subconscious.

Think of your subconscious mind as a bank. Every day and every minute, we are making deposits. Every time someone says something to you, it goes in the bank. Every success and failure goes in the bank. Every skill learned goes in the bank. Every memory goes in the bank. Every action and reaction goes in the bank. Our banks become full of beliefs and attitudes and abilities, which in turn affect our behaviors and actions.

Let's look at an example. Let's say you need to give a fundraising speech at your church. You want to ask people to support the building fund. You start walking up to give the speech, and all of a sudden, your palms get sweaty and you start to get nervous. Your heart is beating a mile a minute. Why?

It could be for a number of reasons. Perhaps subconsciously you are worried that people will judge you for the extra weight you recently put on, so you feel unattractive being in the limelight. It could be that you gave a speech in your past and you lost your place and were embarrassed, and your subconscious makes you fear you'll do it again. It could be you grew up with financial difficulties, and that has impacted how you feel about asking others for money. There are all kinds of reasons that could cause you to be sweating, but we don't often analyze why. Your subconscious is responsible for not only your feelings at this point, but also your bodily functions (sweating and heart beat in this case) that go along with them.

The more we can bring our subconscious "into the light" when making decisions, the more we will feel in control of our choices. As we can grab hold and understand the beliefs that are "making us sweat" – the more ability and freedom we will have to change them.

We, unfortunately, cannot easily dictate new beliefs to our subconscious mind. It is often not enough to say, "Today I am pretty" if your mind actually believes the opposite. Even if you repeat, "Today I am pretty" a thousand times. A positive affirmation like this plants a seed on the conscious level, and may make you feel a bit better temporarily, but to get to the underlying subconscious – the root of your thinking – it frequently takes not just words but effort. Our efforts need to be actions that counter our belief. To use a simple example, if you feel you are not good at math, and want to be, then just saying, "I am good at math" won't really help. You need to educate yourself more. You need to study. You need to do math drills. You need to surround yourself with others who are better than you in math and can help you. You need to make a choice to change your belief by changing your actions. Likewise, if you feel you are not pretty, you can decide one day that indeed you are. But to sustain that new belief, we often need to take steps. In this case, to make yourself feel prettier – perhaps you get a new hairdo or different clothes or start eating healthier -

whatever actions you feel will help you change your belief. You *can* change your beliefs without action, but taking action to consciously change your subconscious often accelerates belief change and makes it more permanent.

So now I need to talk about my husband again. He is an information officer, and some of his staff is responsible for programming computer systems. If something changes in the business, they reprogram to adjust. If there are new laws that require different reporting, again, they reprogram to adjust. Or sometimes they create whole new programs to take on new functionality to meet business needs. Think of all the technology changes in the past twenty plus years, from the Internet to social media to storing data in the cloud. His staff is constantly reprogramming, readjusting, renewing, and realigning.

As we live our lives, wouldn't it be really nice if we could just reprogram to adjust? Wouldn't it be nice if we could take on new challenges by writing new programs?

Well, we can. Let's compare our own mind to one of those computer systems. We have a whole bunch of stuff stored in our hard drive, but only so much brought up at a time in memory and activity. But the hard drive is still processing in the background running things automatically for us. We are constantly storing new things on our hard drive as well. Think of the hard drive as our subconscious mind, and what we see on our screen at any given time as our conscious mind. We may have things programmed in our hard drive that give us autopilot responses. This may include right or wrong ways to cope with different situations, ego defenses to make sure we don't get emotionally hurt, or even ways of rationalizing to make ourselves feel better for not making progress. There are all kinds of subconscious programming at work to affect our choices in life.

And yet, we have the power to reprogram. And even to create new programs. We have the power to decide what we want to get out of life.

The first step in making a CHOICE is to *consciously* decide what we want to change. A particular area in your life wheel? A belief? A behavior? A feeling?

Start by looking at those things that are not making you feel happy or satisfied. Do you have problems matching your income with your expenses? Is your life constrained by the amount and nature of the debt you have? Then you need to start looking at financial choices you are making.

Is something missing in your romantic life? Then it would probably be wise to start looking at some of your personal relationship choices you are making.

Are you stressed out at work? Is your job literally killing you? Then you can start looking at some of the choices you are making regarding your employment and the work relationships there.

And beyond looking at the area(s) in your life that are challenging, look at your beliefs and question which ones may be leading to negative choices. Look at your behaviors and ask yourself if they are bringing you happiness or are getting in the way of it. Behaviors, beliefs, feelings and your choices in each and every area of your life all go hand and hand, but now's the time to do some dissection and *consciously* examine what you want to change - and "why" - to make you feel happier, more satisfied, more fulfilled, or more at peace.

CHOICE

CONSCIOUS Exercise

Let's start this journey with a few questions:

1. What is one change you'd like to **Consciously** make now to get want you want out of life?

2. What is the priority and difficulty of this change? Is it worth it?

3. What subconscious barriers may be in your way, and how can you consciously overcome them?

CHAPTER 5

cHOICE

H is for HOPEFUL

*Hope is the best four-letter word, as it lifts you up
towards a better tomorrow.*

Hopeful:

1. Feeling or inspiring optimism about a future event

2. Cheerfully expectant

3. Positive

4. Buoyant

5. Forwardly enthusiastic

6. Envisioning a good outcome

Imagine two roads in front of you. One is full of darkness and despair, with gnarly trees that seem to hover over you and threaten you harm. Thunder is crashing, and the rain is blinding. The ground is teeming with snakes and poisonous spiders, and beady red eyes from predators glare out at you. You hear growling and see the flash of sharp teeth. If you go down this road, you are well aware that you will likely become lost, scared, tortured, broken, or even killed.

The other road has butterflies flitting around a sea of waving grass. Flowers are blooming and a pleasant aroma is welcoming you. The sun is shining above you, and it is a balmy 72 degrees outside. Gentle deer are grazing, rabbits hopping, birds singing. Ahead of you is even a blackberry bush with ripe, juicy fruit ready to pick. You can see yourself feeling happy, light and excited as you move forward.

Which road would you choose?

All right, I know this seems like a really, really stupid question. The answer is obvious (unless you are suffering from masochism or maybe have a fear of rabbits or hate blackberries). When given a choice this blatant, 99% of us would choose the road with the birds versus the predators.

And yet, in everyday life, we often don't.

Instead, we let ourselves get mired down in what is wrong versus focusing on what we want. We spend years and years trying to heal painful pasts, and yet end up reliving them over and over in our minds. We ask why, why, why? What did I do to deserve this? We make excuses when we fail versus learn and move on. We may even think the world is out to get us. That nobody understands. We feel alone and afraid, angry and defeated. A bad day could turn into a bad week into a bad year.

In short, we feel like we are on that desperate road, full of darkness and despair.

But we don't need to be.

As a big Beatle's fan, the words that come to mind from the song "Let it Be" are simple but powerful:

And when the night is cloudy
There is still a light that shines on me...

Those simple lyrics represent hope. We so often find ourselves walking down the road of despair, when a simple turn will put us back on the path full of light. It's about finding the spark, the inner strength, and the will to follow the light, even in the dark. It's about finding the laughter in our hearts, the lightness in our step, and the latitude in our reach.

Sometimes we can get this hope from our religion, as we imagine God walking with us and holding our hand. Sometimes we get it from the encouragement of others. Sometimes we are inspired by others and see hope for ourselves ("if he can do it, so can I"). Hope is simply a combination of belief and expectation. No matter how we get our hope, it is important to have it, because it needs to shape our decisions. Being hopeful is key to every important choice we make.

How Hope Affects Us

In Jerome Groopman's *The Anatomy of Hope*, he talks about how researchers are learning that a change of mindset – becoming more hopeful – even has the power to alter our neurochemistry. It actually can heal by blocking pain and releasing the brain's endorphins and enkephalins, which mimic the effects of morphine. In some cases, it calms us, and even helps us breathe and physically function better. It can reduce stress and anxiety. A study of law students by psychologists Suzanne Segerstrom of the University of Kentucky and Sandra Sephton of the University of Louisville showed that optimism might even help our immune systems. They tracked 124 students over six months, and found that often the part of their immune system that fights viral infections and some bacterial infections tracked positively with their level of optimism. Other studies have shown how heart transplant patients who are optimistic recover quicker than those who are not. The healing benefits are clear.

But it doesn't stop there. Shane Lopez, author of the book *Making Hope Happen* found that hope triggers a cycle of goodness. People who are hopeful are more able to hold onto a vision despite setbacks. They are more likely to make healthier decisions in the way they eat, exercise, and care for themselves. They are more likely to invest in the future rather than make harmful short-term decisions (like eating that greasy bag of chips or spending money on something unnecessary versus saving for later). Hopeful people stick to their plans better.

Growing up, I often heard the terms "glass half full" or "glass half empty." A glass half full person is the optimist, full of hope, looking on the bright side, while the glass half empty person is the pessimist, looking down the road of despair and finding fault. But did you know that research has also found that seeing the glass half full not only makes you happier and healthier, but also wealthier?

Yep, you heard me. Happy, healthier AND wealthier.

Psychologist Susan Segerstrom found that ten years after graduation, law students who were more optimistic earned on average over $32,000 a year more. It literally *pays* to be hopeful!

Simply stated, expecting and hoping for good things to happen in your life will lead to taking actions that will produce positive results. Expecting gloom and doom to come your way will become self-perpetuating. You will walk the dark path.

In Rhonda Byrne's book, *The Secret*, she expounds on the claim that positive thinking can create life-altering results such as increased health, wealth and happiness. Focusing on the positive attracts positive to us. There are lots and lots of parodies of this work (and yes, some of them are really funny!) but the truth remains, positive thinking is much more likely to generate positive results. While no one is saying to put on blinders to your problems, what this says is to focus on the positive result, not the negatives happening now. Focus on what you want, not what you currently have. Focus on the light at the end of the tunnel, not all the obstacles that may be in the way. It is what we focus on that brings results.

So let me take you back to that glass for a second. I was in a class once and the teacher held up a half full glass. I thought, here we go again, I know this already – she's going to talk about optimism and pessimism. But she didn't. She asked a student to come up and hold the glass. She asked her if it was heavy, and she said no. She told her to go stand in the corner and continue to hold up the glass while she taught the class. As we all watched, we could see the student's discomfort grow as she shifted her weight and even started to stretch out her neck. I could only imagine how an ache in her shoulder started to form from the weight. A weight that seemed so light at first. When it became too much, she asked the teacher if she could put down the glass. The teacher told her, "In a bit." She stood longer, her discomfort continuing to grow. She asked again. The teacher said, "Not yet." Finally, after asking a third time, the teacher let her put down the glass. You could see her relief as she was finally allowed to put the glass on a table.

My teacher told of learning this experiment from a psychologist. The point of it was to teach that the weight of the glass didn't matter as much as how long it was held. If it was just a minute, no problem. An hour? The arm starts to ache. A day? Expect to feel numb and paralyzed. The weight of the glass doesn't change, but the effect of it does. It becomes heavier and heavier. The point is that the stresses and worries in our life are like the glass of water. If we focus on the negatives, they become heavier and heavier, and they become more and more hurtful. Think about them long enough, and they can even be paralyzing and make us incapable of moving forward. Being hopeful means to let go of your stresses and concerns – to put them down as you focus on positive possibilities. Stop thinking about all the wrong, and start focusing on all the right that you have the power to make happen. It doesn't mean the wrong doesn't exist, it means that the more you focus on the positive, the more IT will exist.

The Language of Hope

Okay, time to quote another song. In the play, *Into the Woods*, there's a tune called, "Children will Listen." The song is about what we tell our children and how we role model to them. It cautions us to be very careful in our words and actions. But let's just focus on our words for now. So close your eyes for a second, and imagine these words being sung by the amazing Barbara Streisand (well, you may need to read the words first before you close your eyes, but you get the picture):

Careful the things you say,
Children will listen

While this song is about what we say to our children, it is equally important to be careful about the things we say to each other and even to ourselves.

So let me ask you – is your language filled with fear or is it filled with hope? Is it filled with negatives or positives?

Negative language tells the recipient (someone else, or often ourselves) what cannot be done. It is blaming and accusatory and includes words like won't, can't, not, never, ought to, and should. It is often sarcastic and biting. It compares you to others rather than focuses on being your best self.

Positive language, on the other hand, is focused on what CAN be done. It is encouraging and sounds helpful versus demonizing. It highlights possibilities and purports positive consequences. It is uplifting and caring and filled with hope.

So let's just look at some examples. Read the following ten sentences. As you read them, try to imagine how they would make you feel if someone said them to you right now. Or if you even said them to yourself. We are often our own worst critics, and what we say to ourselves shapes our actions. Are you saying any of these things or similar types of sentences to yourself?

Someone Saying it to You	Saying it to Yourself
1. I think you're going to **fail** at this.	1. I think I'm going to **fail** at this.
2. I **can't** believe how you've let yourself go.	2. I **can't** believe how I've let myself go.
3. You must be **crazy** to think you can do this.	3. I'm **crazy** to think I can do this.
4. You're **not as good** as others.	4. I'm **not as good** as others.
5. You **ought to** stick with what you know versus these **hare brained** ideas.	5. I **ought to** stick with what I know versus these **hare brained** ideas.
6. You're a **terrible** spouse and parent.	6. I'm a **terrible** spouse and parent.
7. You **won't** ever get it right.	7. I **won't** ever get it right.

Yuck, yuck, and more yuck! Are you filling your mind with this crap? Is someone else? There is not an ounce of optimism or hope in any of these seven statements, whether someone else is saying them to you, or you are saying them to yourself.

So what do you do when you are told discouraging words? I *would* suggest you take a wet noodle and whack anyone who says these types of things to you, but I don't want you to get arrested for noodle assault. But what you *can* do is refuse to accept their negativity. You can certainly ask them to rephrase it in a positive light – what do they want you to do? How can you help them better? What good outcome can they describe? But if they can't rephrase it, it is time to tune them out.

And the same goes for your own negativity towards yourself. Imagine a little angel on one shoulder and a little devil on your other shoulder. The angel is whispering encouraging words to you while the devil just points out your faults. This devil just wants to tear you down. He just wants to tell you why you can't do something. He fills your head with excuses and fear. For instance, say you want to find your dream job. Your devil may be stirring you to say to yourself:

- I am too old to start something new.

- I don't have enough education.

- I don't have enough money or I can't get the money I need.

- I don't have the right skills.

- I don't know the right people.

- I can't compete with others.

- I have no experience.

Are you letting the devil shout over your angel? Worse yet, are you letting him just barf all over you with these excuses? Are you having him fill you with fear so you don't move forward? Well, guess what. He doesn't have to control you. In fact, YOU have the power to control him.

Kick his butt to the curb! Whack him with a wet noodle. It's okay, he's just imaginary, so you won't go to jail for assault. **Do not be your own worst enemy**. Be your own best friend. Clear your head of the meanness the devil is spewing.

So, with that in mind, let's take those same sentences in the previous table and turn them around into positive language. Again, read each sentence and let the feelings wash over you. How would it feel for someone to say these things to you? How does it feel to say them to yourself?

Someone Saying it to You	Saying it to Yourself
1. You're going to **succeed** at this.	1. I'm going to **succeed** at this.
2. You are **beautiful** inside and out.	2. I am **beautiful** inside and out.
3. You **can** do this.	3. I **can** do this.
4. You **are** doing **well.**	4. I **am** doing **well**.
5. You **have** interesting ideas.	5. I **have** interesting ideas.
6. You're a **loving** spouse and parent.	6. I'm a **loving** spouse and parent.
7. You **will** get it right.	7. I **will** get it right.

And guess what. Positive self-talk is more than just necessary to move you ahead. It is linked to more happiness in life. In fact, studies have shown that as much as 90% of our happiness is related to our outlook on life, and the conversations we have in our own heads greatly shape this. Fortunately, we can shift our view and perspective by learning to talk to ourselves more positively. In short, we can become more hopeful.

University of Pennsylvania Psychology Professor Martin Seligman studied the ways people explain events in their lives. He found that pessimists tend to form worldviews around negative events and explained away anything good that happened to them. Optimists, on the other hand, distanced themselves from negative events and embraced the positive. They were more likely to say anything negative was temporary and fixable, while the pessimist viewed it as a permanent state.

Scientists have found that there is a genetic predisposition to being optimistic versus pessimistic. We are born with certain inclinations. We cannot change our genetic code, or our predispositions. However, much of our worldview can be nurtured and shaped, not just by how we are raised but also by the people we choose to have in our lives in later years. If we surround ourselves with people who uplift us, we will begin to feel more positive. If we surround ourselves with support and love, we will feel more capable and willing to take risks and reach out. But the most powerful shaper of this view is ourselves. So even if you've been pessimistic your whole life, and even if you've been discouraged by others, it is possible to become happier by shifting your own perspective. It is possible to renew and refresh your thinking and self-talk. You can go from a world of can't, won't, and don't, to a world of can, will, and do.

We can start the cycle of better self-talk in small ways. If you miss your bus, instead of kicking yourself and treating it as a catastrophe, think about ways to make productive use of your time while you wait for the next one. If you lost a business deal, focus on the learning that you can use as you talk with another potential client. Tripped and fell? Don't yell at yourself for being klutzy; instead just say "oops" and move on. Minimize the bad and maximize the good you have in life. Remind yourself of all the things you can appreciate (A hot shower? A meal? A friend? The list goes on and on). The more you appreciate what you do have in life, versus focusing on what you don't have, the more you begin to create a positive mindset and become more hopeful.

There is a whole field called Neuro-linguistic programming (NLP) which is an approach to communication, personal development and psychotherapy. It was created by Richard Bandler and John Grinder in the 1970's as they looked at the connection between neurological processes, language, and behavioral patterns learned through experience (programming), and how we can reprogram ourselves to achieve the goals we want in life. Through it they offered the use of transformational grammar to yield a more positive and specific view of what a person wants and feels. There is a lot more to NLP than the language component, yet this self-communication piece is vital. By challenging our linguistic distortions, specifying our generalizations, and even understanding what we avoid saying to ourselves, we can paint a clearer and more positive picture of where we want to go.

In short, the clearer and more specific we are with what we positively want, and the more effective we are at communicating that to ourselves and others, the more likely we are to get it.

So now let's talk a bit more about how to be **Hopeful** in our choices. Even after picking an area in our life to change, we often emphasize what we don't want any more versus focusing on what we DO want. Here are some examples:

1) I want to stop fighting in my marriage

2) I need to lose weight

3) I'm tired of not being able to afford anything

4) I hate my job and want to quit

5) I can't seem to find anyone good to date

6) I feel stressed all the time

7) I am overwhelmed with too many things to get done.

8) I gamble too much.

9) My sex life stinks

10) I can't seem to get motivated to do anything.

By now, with all the discussion about positive language, perhaps you recognize some key no-no words in these sentences. Let's look at them again:

1) I want to stop **fighting** in my marriage

2) I want to **lose** weight

3) I'm **tired** of **not** being able to afford anything

4) I **hate** my job and want to **quit**

5) I **can't** seem to find anyone good to date

6) I **can't** seem to get motivated to take the first step

7) I **feel stressed** all the time

8) I am **overwhelmed** with too many things to get done

9) I **gamble** too much

10) My sex life **stinks**

These types of sentences actually repel what you'd like versus attract you to it. Yes, they actually work backwards! When you say you want to stop fighting in your marriage, your brain just thinks of the bold "fighting" in my marriage, "fighting" in my marriage, "fighting" in my marriage. And guess what you attract? Fighting! When you talk about losing weight, your brain might just read the word "losing." Losing, losing, losing….do you really want to focus on being a loser?

Do you tell yourself you want to: Lose weight?

Or do you want to: Become healthier?

If you want to lose weight, you may end up considering some options that are unhealthy: fad diets, not eating enough, reliance on pills for quick but unsustainable loss. Even saying you are "going *on* a diet" connotes that someday you will "go *off* a diet." And then what?

However, if you consciously decide to "become healthier," your options will become different. You are more likely to decide to start eating healthier for the rest of your life, and to start an exercise regimen. So we must not only consciously determine what we want to change, but we need to be very careful in defining it so it is truly a positive change. We need to make sure the choice we end up making moves us towards a direction we want.

Taking some other examples on this list, do you want your brain to think you are not able to afford, that you hate, that you're a quitter, and that you can't? Do you want your brain to continue to feel stressed, overwhelmed and have you gamble? Do you want to stink?

So let's rephrase these all to be hopeful. To be positive. To send a clear message to our brains of what we DO want.

But before we do, let's talk a little more about how our brain works. Our brain reads a sentence or hears a sentence, and interprets it as a truism. So the more we talk and form our hopeful desires, *as if we've already attained them*, the more powerful they will be. This doesn't mean we HAVE attained them yet, but it tells us what we are aiming for as if it were already a reality. And then our brain works harder to actually make it a reality.

I have worked with a lot of companies and people on their visions, and I always encourage them to put them in the present tense. We attract what we say. So if we say: "We ARE the number one health care company" or: "I HAVE a wonderful relationship with my spouse," then we are more likely to find the actions to make that happen.

So let's look at those areas in our life to change, and put the hopeful, positive, and present tense spin on them:

1) I have a peaceful and supportive marriage

2) I am healthy

3) I am able to afford nice things

4) I have a fulfilling career

5) A great person is out there excited to date me

6) I am motivated to take the first step

7) I feel relaxed and calm

8) I feel balanced

9) I have healthy recreational habits

10) My sex life is AWESOME

Do you see how powerful and positive these statements are? Writing and reading them as if they already exist often fills a person with hopefulness in the possibility that they can indeed become true. So after you consciously choose what to change in your life, be **Hopeful** in how you state it. For every single change you decide to take on from now on in life, keep this hope. Use this hope. Live with hope.

cHoice

HOPEFUL Exercise

1) For what you've **Consciously** decided to change, what do you **Hope** to achieve?

2) How can you state this as positively as possible?

3) Make sure to put it in the present tense below:

CHAPTER 6

CH**O**ICE

O is for OPEN

*Open your heart, open your mind, open your spirit,
and open your eyes to the wonderful
possibilities life has to offer.*

<u>Open:</u>

1. Allowing access, passage or view through

2. Not closed, not blocked up

3. Unfastened, exposed, uncovered

4. Free of limitations

5. Undecided, unsettled, unresolved

6. Unbiased, unprejudiced, objective

If I asked you if you were open minded, what would you say? If I asked if you were open to possibilities, how might you answer?

Let's raise the stakes. Assume I asked if you thought it was possible to get promoted to a high level in your company? To travel the world? To have fame? To love your work? Or even to find someone who would love and support you? Do you think those possibilities are just pipe dreams? Can you honestly say that you would embrace those ideas and be open to actually thinking you can make them happen?

I think we all like to feel that we are open-minded, with a positive attitude and that we have the potential to achieve our dreams. But if we explore deeper, do we simply say we believe that we are open or are we truly open to new and exciting possibilities?

I know you have heard the expression, "actions speak louder than words." It is true. A friend of mine was a psychiatrist and one of his favorite expressions was, "Listen to what a person says but pay more attention to what they do." I asked him to explain what he meant. He said that a person would often say what they think the other person wants to hear. But their actions are often in conflict with what they say. In the long run, a person's actions will be a reflection of their deep beliefs.

So even if you profess to being open to new possibilities, the proof of the pudding is in your actions. If your actions are based on self-limiting beliefs, on maintaining the status quo rather than in pursuit of your dreams, then you are not open to what's possible in life. Your beliefs will become self-fulfilling. You will not enjoy all that life has to offer.

We are often tied to the way we have always done things – to the way we think things are supposed to work. Let me explain by telling a little story about an experience I recently had at a motel. I was travelling with my family and had booked two rooms at a motel. We checked in, got the room key cards (those cards that look like a credit card and are encoded with the room number), unloaded the car and headed for the rooms.

We made our way to the first room where I inserted the key card. The green light lit up indicating the locking mechanism was unlocked, and I pushed down on the handle and opened the door. I unloaded the appropriate luggage and then walked to the other room just a few doors down the hall.

I inserted the key card and the green light lit up indicating the locking mechanism was unlocked. I pushed down on the handle and nothing happened. The handle would not move. I pushed down again, but nothing moved. I inserted the key card again, got the green light and pushed down – a bit harder this time. Still no movement.

I started thinking about what could be wrong. Could the room attendant have somehow locked the room so it was not accessible? Could the prior guest still be in the room?

I have operated motel doors like this dozens of times. Insert the card, get the green light and push down on the handle to open the door. So I tried one more time. Even though I had the green light, when I pushed down on the handle, it would not budge.

I was becoming irritated. I mean, I do not normally swear (well, maybe a bit), but I was thinking 'WTF – What the F*ck?' at this point. I do not like wasting time and I had some appointments that I needed to keep. I glanced around and saw that the room attendant was still in the hall cleaning other rooms. So I went to the room where she was working. I was about to knock on the door when she came out to her cart to get some fresh supplies.

I explained what was happening. She smiled and said, "Some of the handles were installed upside down. Just lift the handle."

I went back to the room, inserted the card, saw the green light and lifted up on the handle. Presto, the door opened like magic. And presto, I actually also felt a little stupid.

I stopped and reflected on what had happened. I realized that all the other times I had opened motel doors, the handle operated by pushing down on it. Since I have been conditioned to pushing down on the handle, it never occurred to me (duh!) that the door might open if I pulled up on the handle. I was totally not open to the door working other than the way I expected.

I believe we get trapped into thinking that things work one way and only one way. When we "know" the right answer, we are not open to seeing things from any other perspective.

Most people who claim to be open to new and exciting possibilities are not. I suspect that right now you are thinking that you are certainly the exception. But let me share with you the results of an experiment carried out by Dr. George Land. This experiment was originally designed for NASA to test the imagination of scientists and astronauts. Dr. Land thought the test was very simple and he wondered how children would score on it. As an experiment, he decided to administer it to children and track the results. So he selected about 1,600 children between the ages of 4 and 5 years old to take the test.

The results were amazing. Before you read further, take a guess to see how many children scored high in creativity. 50%? 60%? 80%? If you are like me, you missed it by a wide margin. A full 98% of the 4-5 year-old children tested high in creativity. Read that again: 98%. The creativity we have when we are young is astounding.

Dr. Land then decided to do what is called a longitudinal study - that is, to extend the test over a period of years and track the results. So they tested the same children again when they were 10 years old. Want to guess the results? By that time, the children that tested high in creativity had dropped to only 30%.

The next test in the study was conducted when the children were 15 years old. By now, you know to expect a further drop in creativity or possibility thinking. You are correct. At age 15, only 12% of the children tested high in creativity.

But Dr. Land did not stop there. He also tested over 280,000 adults ages 25+ using the same test that he had administered to the children. The results were shocking. Only 2% of adults tested as being creative.

Yikes! Where o' where did our creativity go? Did aliens highjack it? Did we drop piles of it along the street as we walked? Did we give it up for lent or trade it in for a new car? Unfortunately, we DID willingly give it up. We actually learned how to give it up. And here's how.

As Dr. Land explains, there are two types of thinking that goes on in our brains. One he calls divergent thinking – which involves the imagination and possibility thinking. Now you can understand why young children scored so high. They were not inhibited by self-limiting beliefs. The other type of thinking he describes as convergent thinking – which includes making judgments, decisions, and testing.

Dr. Land describes divergent thinking as equivalent to the accelerator in a car and convergent thinking as equivalent to the brakes. When we engage in divergent thinking, we can zoom ahead. When we engage in convergent thinking, we put the brakes on ideas and possibilities.

If you are an adult, actually if you are over 15, there is an extremely high possibility that you have been taught, trained, and conditioned to engage in convergent thinking. You are simply not open to possibilities.

It might be helpful to examine how our possibility thinking gets suppressed. Part of it is our educational system and part is our culture. Our educational system teaches us to search for THE right answer. It teaches us to fit in with the normal, to color in the lines, to always do what is acceptable. Our culture teaches us that success comes from doing what is expected, fitting in, and living within acceptable boundaries.

The other part is the natural conflict within our brain. As soon as we engage in divergent or possibility thinking, our brains start evaluating and judging our ideas. The basic function of our brain is to keep us safe and alive. Our brain tries to help us avoid things that would be dangerous to us. So anytime we think about activities that are new and different, our brain engages in convergent thinking - making judgments about whether that activity is dangerous, testing the idea for possible danger, and making decisions about whether we should continue with the new idea or drop it.

What Dr. Land concluded was that "non-creative behavior is learned." We have learned how to suppress our divergent or possibility thinking. However, if we can learn something, we can also un-learn it.

So I started by asking if you were open to possibilities. Of course I cannot know how you may have answered my question originally. I hope by now that you realize that so much of our thinking is not open. So much is based on convergent thinking. And convergent thinking is characterized by judgment, criticizing and censoring.

Of course there are degrees of being open. We can be open about small things. But as we move from the mundane to the important, we are more likely to engage in convergent thinking - thinking that cuts off possibilities.

For example, we might be open to trying different kinds of foods. We might be open to watching different movies or reading a wide range of books. But when it comes to life changing decisions, we become more closed.

What Mindset Do You Have?

Dr. Land's study was groundbreaking in determining how much we learn to sacrifice possibilities or not even consider them. On how much we limit ourselves from the start versus give ourselves room to imagine. He showed us how we put chains on our ideas and creativity over the years, and the difficulty we have as adults in removing these self-imposed shackles.

Stanford University PhD. Psychologist, Carol Dweck, conducted another great study that looked at our ability to be open to possibilities. Dr. Dweck is the author of *Mindset: The New Psychology of Success*. The book is based on decades of research about why some people are successful and others struggle. The main theme is that people tend to have either a fixed mindset or a growth mindset.

A person with a predominately fixed mindset believes they are born with a certain level of talent and intelligence that will basically control how far they can go in life. A person with a fixed mindset generally relies on their natural abilities and believes if too much effort is needed to exceed these abilities, it is better to give up.

A person with a predominately growth mindset believes talent and intelligence are not what limits them. They strongly believe that effort is the determining factor in their success. If they put in enough effort, they will reach their goals.

The fixed or growth mindset is not either/or. Even those who score high on growth mindset have a touch of fixed mindset in their personality. And the reverse is also true.

The reason this is important is because your mindset has a significant bearing on what you achieve in life. A growth mindset can be thought of as being open, while a fixed mindset can be thought of as being closed.

Let's look a little closer at some of the differences that occur because of our different mindsets. Dr. Dweck did an experiment with a group of 10-year-old students. She gave them a quiz that she knew was too difficult for their grade level. One group expressed appreciation for the challenge, saying things like, "I love a good challenge" or "I was hoping to learn something new." She classified these students as having a growth mindset.

The other students viewed the test totally different. They thought it was "tragic, a disaster, their intelligence had been tested and they came up short." This group she classified as having a fixed mindset.

The most interesting thing that came out of the experiment was what the students with a fixed mindset said about how they would handle a difficult test in the future. Some said they would resort to cheating the next time. Others said they would try to find someone who did worse than they did – they wanted to be better by comparison.

The conclusion was that those with a fixed mindset would run from a challenge or seek a way to negatively deal with it.

If you try to avoid difficulty, what are the chances that you will achieve your goals? Will you really be open to making the best choice?

In another experiment, Ms. Dweck tested a group of students and found some stark differences between the beliefs of those with a fixed mindset and those with a growth mindset. She summarized their beliefs. For the fixed mindset, 1) They wanted to look smart at all times and at all cost. They tried to avoid looking dumb. 2) They viewed effort as bad. If you had to put too much effort into a task, you must be lacking in ability. 3) They viewed setbacks or failures as a measure that revealed their limitations. Setbacks and failures were disasters.

For the growth mindsets: 1) They valued learning at all times and all costs. Learning was the ultimate goal. 2) Effort was what activated their ability, so the more effort, the more their abilities grew. 3) Mistakes and failure were a natural part of learning. When they made a mistake, they capitalized on it. They viewed it as a way to grow and expand.

I am hoping you are beginning to see the benefits of being open – of having a growth mindset.

If you are thinking that you might have a fixed mindset and are not open to learning and growing from mistakes, take heart. You can learn to adopt a growth mindset. There is a very simple change you can make that will greatly improve your mindset. It is taken from a high school in Chicago. When they administer the test to see if a student passed from high school, they do not give a failing grade. The student passes or gets a grade of "Not Yet". This has made all the difference in the world to those students who were struggling. Instead of the stigma of getting a failing grade, their grade simply acknowledges that they have not yet mastered what they need to. It also gives them the belief that they can.

If you have a growth mindset, you are open to new possibilities. You do not try to avoid tough situations, and you do not hide your deficiencies. You embrace the need for effort, you treat all setbacks as learning opportunities and you take great comfort in "Not Yet."

"Not Yet" means that you are still in the game.

Would you let a 7 year-old have control of your life?

If I asked this question, I have no doubt the majority of people would answer, "No way in hell would I allow a 7 year-old to have control of my life."

And yet, we let the beliefs implanted in us when we are young often control our lives. We touched on beliefs during the third chapter. Your beliefs are a state of mind in which we regard something - an assumption or a conviction - to be true.

Most of our beliefs are formed in our childhood. They are planted by our parents and other relatives, our educational and spiritual teachers and by our peers. At that age, we accept many things as truths because we have no good reason to doubt them. We are taught about our limits, we are taught about money, success and a host of other things that we carry into our adult life - often without questioning.

But you do have a choice. You can be open to questioning those beliefs. You can examine them to see if they are true and valid. You can take control of your life from the beliefs instilled in you when you were just 7 years old.

Socrates once said, "An unexamined life is not worth living." Have you really examined your life? Are you open to examining your life, to testing those beliefs that control your life?

So much of what we do is automatic. We react in a certain way to an event. When that event happens again, we react the same way. Soon we have created a habit. We talked about habits earlier, but in this chapter, let's talk specifically about how they can close us off to being open. The majority of things that happen in life happen repeatedly.

For something simple, like lunch, that is okay. If you want to pick a favorite restaurant because you really like their Asian salad, and you "gotta have it," it's not a bad habit to have. We don't always have to be open to other possibilities, especially if we like the current ones and they're healthy for us. But let's look at some other areas of life where we have choices but have never stopped to question if we are responding in the best way. Take a simple example that your spouse says something you find negative. What is your knee-jerk reaction? Do you snap back with a sharp cutting attack? Do you silently vow to even the score? Do you slam the door and walk out? You probably have a predictable habitual response to this and dozens of other things that happen daily.

My question to you is this: Is this behavior serving you well? Is it leading you toward what you want in life? If not, are you **open** to questioning what you could/should do that would give you the results you want?

How Being Closed to New Beliefs Limits Us

Circle Back to the Motel...

I want to return to the problem with the motel door lock. When I first tried the lock, I was not open to the fact that my beliefs about how the door should work could be wrong.

After I had tried 3 or 4 times, I realized that continuing the same behavior was not going to give me different results. But I was still not open to the idea that I might be doing something wrong. In fact, I was certain that there was something wrong with the lock.

My belief that it was not MY thinking or my actions that might be the problem was what allowed me to seek help.

Once I was told by an authority figure how to solve the problem, I had no difficulty accepting the solution.

Now this was a rather minor issue and I had no personal identity invested in how I thought the lock should work. Proving my theory about how the lock should work was not going to make me question my core beliefs. It was not that serious.

We hold very fixed beliefs about plenty of ideas and issues in life, and unfortunately, these beliefs don't always serve us well. But we are not open to questioning them. Most of these beliefs revolve around religion, politics and cultural values that were mostly instilled in our subconscious mind when we were children. We hold many beliefs about what is right and what is wrong. Those beliefs become entrenched as our core values and are not subject to examination. We have made countless choices based on those core values and because we have made so many choices, our actions become habit.

Most of our decisions are made without thinking. Even though we have free will. Even though we have a choice about things, we rarely exercise that choice.

Our brains are focused on survival. Part of that means we need to live with a certain amount of efficiency. If we expend too much energy making routine decisions, if we open ourselves to possibilities to every single decision we make, we would never get enough done. So once we have made a decision a few times, it becomes habit and our brain defaults to doing what we have done in the past.

But that means that we are generally not **open** to making new and better choices. We make choices based on what we have done in the past.

So where do you draw the line? How do you decide *when* to be more open? Well, easy. You've already done it. You did it when you answered the questions in earlier chapters about where you consciously wanted to make a change, how important these changes were to you, and how to address them with a hopeful versus fearful mindset.

But okay, now you may be asking, HOW do I become more open? Even when I have decided that it is a priority to do so, and that I'm going to open my arms in hope to possibilities, just how do I go about doing this?

Ways to Be More Open to Possibilities

Well, don't worry. I'm not going to leave you hanging. There are a lot of different ways to open your mind to new ideas and possibilities. Let's look at seven of these here.

1) BRAINSTORMING
An oldie but a goodie.

The first rule of brainstorming is to list all the possibilities without evaluating any of them. In other words, engage fully in divergent or possibility thinking and do not allow any convergent thoughts - judgment, criticism or censoring to enter the picture. Allow your imagination to run wild. Engage in possibility thinking. Be fully open to options.

For instance, instead of thinking of all the reasons why you *cannot* achieve your financial goals, start making a list of all the various ways you *could* achieve your financial goals. The longer list you make, the better. Open your mind to even the most "ridiculous" possibilities. Don't limit yourself for any reason. Even if you think the idea is not worth considering, put it on the list.

I have facilitated enough brainstorming sessions to see that the most absurd ideas sometimes end up being the greatest ones. So just get the idea out there.

2) PARADOXICAL BRAINSTORMING
Let's go really crazy!

With Paradoxical Brainstorming, instead of trying to think of all the ways you could achieve your goal, think of ways that would actually keep you from meeting your goal. Want to become healthier? Paradoxical brainstorming would have you eating ice cream every night. Or becoming a couch potato. Or snorting cocaine. Or many other ways to become unhealthy. Want to have a child? Well, then obviously you need to become celibate. Or use triple birth control. Or go on a trip in the middle of the ocean by yourself so no one is near you. Want to meet new friends? Sit in your room every night. Talk nasty to people. Blow your nose in their shirts.

The idea is to have lots of fun thinking of all different ways you can sabotage getting to your goal. Go wild and be a lunatic! Just think of the stupidest ideas on how not to get your goal met. Think of ways that clearly would not work. Just like with brainstorming, when you engage in Paradoxical Brainstorming, you do not want to do any evaluation. Just get down on paper as many bad ideas as you can. Strive for at least 20 ways that clearly would not help you achieve your goal.

If you do this correctly, you will free your mind from the pressure of thinking of creative or clever ideas to achieve your goals. As you relieve the pressure to perform, your mind is free to be creative. It can make connections that you might never have been able to make.

Once you have at least 20 crazy ideas that clearly will not work, you should look at each idea and try to turn it around. Let me give you an example. Suppose your goal was to get rid of credit card debt. And one of your crazy ideas was "take a trip around the world and charge it to the highest interest rate card." You could turn it around by saying, "Take a trip down memory lane" or "Start enjoying the simple pleasures in life that cost nothing." So what started out as a crazy idea – "taking an expensive trip around the world" actually gets transformed into a very positive idea (or two) to get rid of credit card debt or at least not rack up more. Chances are you might not have thought of these unless you engaged in paradoxical brainstorming.

3) ANSWER WHY, WHY, WHY, WHY...
Be like an annoying little kid.

Little three and four year-old kids ask why a lot. Now, while we think at times this can get super annoying, it really is a great technique for being open. Because those little kids are not locked in to any certain way of doing something. They are not assuming it has to be a certain way. When they ask why, they are genuinely curious.

Let's show you a typical kid/parent conversation:

"Wash up, Johnnie – dinner is almost ready."

"Why do I need to wash up?"

"To eliminate germs."

"Why do I need to eliminate germs?"

"Because they're bad for you."

"Why are they bad for me?"

"Because they can make you sick."

"Why will they make me sick?"

"Because they just will. Now go wash up!"

You can just hear the frustration in the parent's voice as their child questions them. But the kid is actually asking valid questions. Does he really need to wash up? Will germs really make him sick? Or is this just an assumption? Now, I'm not saying to never wash up. But here's an example where the more we question why, the more we can test our assumptions. Why does it have to be that way?

In fact, Johnnie may have a point. Recent studies have shown that children with a prolonged exposure to antibacterial soap have a higher chance of developing allergies and hay fever. Scientists speculate that this could be a result of reduced exposure to bacteria, **which could be necessary for proper immune system functioning and development**. Hmmmm...no wonder we never see the character Pig Pen from the Peanuts sneezing – he's allergy free! All kidding aside, the point is, being open and curious helps us test our assumptions.

Questioning helps us challenge the status quo. It helps us look at different options and become more open in our thinking. When you are faced with making a choice, ask yourself, "Why should I take this course of action?" And once you have decided on an answer, ask again, "And why is that so?" In other words, ask again if your reasoning is valid. You can and should continue asking why for a couple more rounds. This might seem a little silly, but trust me. If you do this right, you will gain some new insights into your behavior. Just keep asking "Why," and you are bound to get some "ahas," and even some new alternatives.

Another way to use "Why" is by forcing yourself to answer differently to the same question. Let's say that you are not happy at work and are contemplating looking for a new job. Ask the question: Why am I looking for a new job? Your answer might be, "Because my stress level is too high and my pay is too low." Again you ask: Why should I get a new job? You cannot give the same answer. You could say, "Because the family is growing and I need to earn more money to support them." Again, ask why? This time you might think, "Because maybe I really want to start my own business versus work for someone else." Continue asking why you're looking for a new job. Continue thinking of different reasons and perspectives. Test your initial assumptions as to why you really want a new job. The more you ask why, the more your mind will be open to new and exciting (or scary) ideas and even some eye-opening moments.

And finally, a third way to use "Why" is to change it into "Why Not?" If you think you have an idea, but then dismiss it too soon, ask yourself "Why Not?" What's really behind your objection to that idea, thought, possibility? Why not keep that idea open for consideration? Why not explore? Why not take a chance? Why not be adventurous? Why not have the chutzpah to put yourself "out there" a bit more? Why not keep things on the list of possibilities, at least for now? As we move into the next phases of making a CHOICE, there will be room for determining which ideas may be better than others, but for now, don't dismiss anything too early.

So, be sure to ask "why" and also "why not?" They are both key in keeping options open.

4) LEAVE YOUR ANXIETIES BEHIND
Be like an uninhibited child.

If I asked you to draw a picture of a friend and give it to them, would you do it? Okay, if you are an artist, perhaps this is an easy question, but for those of us who draw in stick figures, we might feel mortified. Embarrassed. Silly. We would be afraid of being judged as inept. So we shy away from trying.

This method has you actually trying to be inept! Well, not really, but at least not worrying about it. A way to increase openness is to go out and do something just a little bit beyond your comfort level. It doesn't need to be anything to do with the choice you are currently making. This is just to open your mind to feeling okay with being a bit silly. A bit not-so-perfect. A bit willing to try anything. So, if you think you can't draw, draw a picture of something and share it. If you think you don't write well, write a poem and give it to someone. Don't like your singing voice? Sing out "pass the potatoes please" at the dinner table. If people think you are weird, who cares? Let it brush off you. You'll be surprised how trying something new and out of your comfort zone makes you more open to trying other things as well.

Professor Robert McKim was the head of Research Design at Stanford University back in the 1980s. He created some exercises that were quite effective in getting people to be more creative and open.

In one exercise he conducted at conferences, he had people draw a picture of the person sitting next to them. He only gave them 30 seconds to complete the picture. So how did people react? For starters, most people were nervous because they didn't consider themselves artists, and even more nervous only with the time limit of only 30 seconds to try to draw someone else. The reaction was quite predictable. Most people were reluctant to show their masterpiece to the person sitting next to them. And when they did, you could hear a lot of, "I'm sorry. I know you don't look like that." There was a lot of laughter and occasionally some, "Oh, geez, is that the best you could do?" As adults we are afraid to show our work. We are afraid to be judged. But Mr. McKim also did the experiment with very young children. What do you think they did when asked to show their artwork to their neighbor? They were excited to share. They did not feel any reluctance. They were quite proud of what they had done and eager to exhibit their work.

So it is helpful to think like a child. Children are eager to learn and to share. They do not let their fear of being judged stop them from fully engaging in any activity. When asked to draw, children do not think of it as work, they think of it as play. So no matter what new activities you are undertaking, take a playful attitude toward it. A good question to ask yourself, "How would a 5-year-old child handle this?"

If you can put yourself in the place of a 5-year-old, you will give up your rigid beliefs about what you should do. You will start to think with an expanded view of possibilities. So just for a moment, think like a child.

Now let's look at a different situation. Have you ever been around a two-year old when they opened Christmas or birthday presents? If you have, then there is no doubt that you have seen one unwrap a $50 toy and immediately begin to play with the wrapping paper or the box instead of the toy.

Children can often have more fun with the box or the wrapping paper than with the expensive toy. Now I am not suggesting that you copy this behavior. What I am suggesting is that you adopt the curiosity of a child. When presented with a new choice, ask: What is it? What can I do with it? What else can I do with it?

Instead of accepting that the wrapping paper of the box the toy came in is trash, ask: Is there any other thing I can do with these items? Learn to ask how else can you look at things. Are there different uses that you have not yet considered? How might a child look at this and figure out ideas? Be uninhibited like that child!

5)   STOP SAYING NIH: "Not Invented Here"
Or translate it to "Nothing Is Have-to."

In business there is a common reaction to new ideas that come from outside the company or group. It goes by the shorthand NIH, "Not Invented Here." When someone from outside the company comes up with an idea to save money or improve operations/working conditions, the knee jerk reaction is it won't work. The underlying thought behind the NIH is that those closest to the problem know what works best, and people from the outside don't understand it enough to know this.

That is not always the case. At times someone with a different perspective can see things that those on the inside can't see.

Let me give you an example. Sal Khan was an investment banker with no formal background in education. People told him you "have to" have an education background in order to have an academy. People told him you "have to" teach face to face to be effective. People told him you "have to" do it the traditional way.

Sal Khan founded the Khan Academy, the most successful online learning platform there is. The YouTube channel has over 2,000,000 subscribers and as of January 2015, the Khan Academy videos have been viewed over 513 million times.

If he had not been open to doing things a new way, the Khan Academy would not exist. If he had listened to all those "have-to" people, he would not have created his highly successful academy.

So when you catch yourself saying, "It won't work." Turn it around. Instead ask, "What would I need to do to make it work?" "How can I shift my approach so that it will work?" And change the meaning of NIH from "Not Invented Here" to "Nothing is Have-to." NOTHING is HAVE to. You don't have to do it any particular way, even if it's always been done that way. Think of different ways to make something work – open your mind and heart to possibilities.

6) USE "IF I DID KNOW...."
You know more than you think you do.

It is sometimes easier to let someone else decide for you. Have you ever been in a situation where you did not know what you wanted to do or what you should do? Let's take a rather simple example. Say you are planning to go to dinner with a loved one and you are trying to decide which restaurant to go to. Your partner asks, "Where should we go?" And then you answer, "I don't know. Where would YOU like to go?"

Instead of replying, "I don't know," ask your self this simple question, "If I did know, where would we go?" So the exercise is simple, instead of avoiding the question by saying, "I don't know," force your self to answer the question. If you ask yourself, "If I did know, what would the answer be?" you will open up some new possible answers. This can be used for bigger issues as well, like, "If I did know what career I'd like to pursue, what would the answer be?" "If I did know whether this person is worth dating, what would the answer be?" "If I did know how to expand my business successfully, what would the answer be?"

The mere method of forcing yourself to think of possibilities will lead you to.... think of possibilities.

7) USE "LIKE" MORE TO OPEN YOUR THINKING
You're Going to "Like" This One!

We use the word "like" a lot. We might "like" something in Facebook. We might like the fit of the pants we're wearing. And many of us use the word "like" as a filler word when we talk. Like, you know what I mean? So now we are going to cover another way to use "like," but this time focusing in on how to use it to open possibilities.

Take the choice you want to make and list everything about it that you might like. New house decision? What would you like about a new house? New job? What would you like? New relationship? What would you like him or her to look like, feel like, act like, or even smell like? Use all your senses to paint your "like" picture.

Let's take the example of a new healthy habit. What would you like? To feel good? To have six pack abs? To fit it in your schedule? To feel in control? To enjoy it? To get compliments? To live longer? To have better skin? To feel more energetic? To sleep better? To throw away medications since they are not needed anymore? To do it on your own? To do it with the support of a group? To breathe easier? To role model to your children better? To reduce your insurance bills? To look better in clothes (or out of them!)? To feel confident? To attract others more? To save money? What would you like to feel, taste, hear, see, touch, or smell? Opening up your mind and heart to your "likes" will help you open up possibilities to pursue that might meet those likes.

Be conscious, be hopeful, be open.

Hopefully by all these methods, you are getting the picture. Being open means that you think differently, you ask different questions, you ask deeper questions, and you give up acting out of habit. Being open means that you take control of your life by examining new possibilities on what to do and how to move forward toward the goal you want.

Einstein said, "Imagination is more important than knowledge." Let me say the same thing just a bit differently. Being open - engaging in divergent thinking - is the key to making better choices. And making better choices is the key to a better life.

So now that we've opened your mind to the possibility of openness (crazy, eh?), and have even learned ways to be more open, you are ready for the next step.

CH**O**ICE

OPEN Exercise

1) For what you've **Consciously** decided to change, and with **Hopefulness** in mind, what possibilities are you **Open** to?

2) Take one or more of the "open your mind to possibilities" techniques – brainstorming, paradoxical brainstorming, asking why repeatedly, etc. and apply this to what you want to change.

3) Come up with at least 3 different ways to change, but the more the merrier. Be ridiculous! Be crazy. Be exploratory. Be **open** to possibilities of how to get what you want out of life.

CHAPTER 7

CHOICE

I is for INFORMED

*Information helps shape our choices
like a potter's hands shape clay*

Informed:

1. To have knowledge of a fact or circumstance

2. Supplied with data on a particular matter or subject

3. Educated and cognizant

4. Trained, instructed, shown, told

5. Filled in, brought up to date, notified

6. Well versed and learned, disclosed

When facing a choice and you consider the word "Informed," what comes to mind?

For many of us who prefer to act spontaneously or impulsively – with a "devil may care" attitude, researching information may seem a drag. A snoozer. BORING. Pain in the behind side. Tedious. Maybe even not worth our time.

Plus, if you were properly informed, how do we even know this would lead to the best choice? And what does properly informed even mean? Do you need to have all available information? Or is having 75 or 80% of the information about a choice adequately informed?

All this talk about making informed choices is great. But life often happens in a hurry. Sometimes, you don't have the luxury of collecting information, weighing possible outcomes and arriving at an informed decision. There are times your choices come with rigid time constraints.

For instance, there are certain activities where you are forced to make quick decisions. When you are driving on a residential street and a child runs from behind a parked car, you do not have time to become informed about the possible consequences of your actions. You react by slamming on the brakes or turning sharply. You may risk getting hit from behind or crashing into a car parked on the side of the street. You had to make an immediate decision as to what to do to avoid the child.

The great majority of our decisions in life are made without researching information. We just don't have time to research everything on a day-to-day basis. We act on very limited information, and most of the time, that's good enough. For instance, I don't need to research methods of cleaning my cat's vomit. I just take out the rags, water, cleansers, and do it. I COULD research the best way to do this, but I don't. What I do is good enough. This is because cleaning the cat throw up is not going to impact my life significantly. Yes, I will avoid stepping in it by cleaning. And I will avoid the house looking messy. But these consequences are not going to significantly add to my happiness in life. So I think my current knowledge is good enough for resolving the issue.

But if we are going to make better choices about areas that DO impact us more, we must have adequate information.

There are four steps to being properly informed. Here they are in a nutshell:

1. We must know *what* information to collect.

2. We need to know *how* to collect the information we will need.

3. We must be able to *validate* the information we collect.

4. And lastly, we need to know *how much* information is enough.

Let's look at these one by one.

1) WHAT INFORMATION TO COLLECT

Narrowing down the information you collect so that it helps you make better choices should be your goal when you begin. And the information to collect is highly dependent on what change you want to make, and what possibilities you are open to consider.

In Chapter 10, you will find some applied examples of CHOICE. These are topics most people face at some time in their lives. Let's take two of them – career and marriage problems. If we conducted a Google search on Career Problems we would find about 509 million possible sources of information. If we did the same search on Marriage Problems, we would be shown about 209 million sources of information. It is quite obvious that before we could explore all those sources of information, the problem would no longer exist…because, to be blunt, with all the years it would take to read millions of sources, WE would no longer exist.

So how do we know what information to seek? Let's look at career first. Start by researching into the outcome you want – what you hope to get. Next, delve into the possibilities you are willing to consider for the change you want to make. Is a new job within the same company a consideration? What about a new company? What about a new company in a new location? What about a new career focus? What information you need to find is shaped on the outcome you hope to achieve and the possibilities you are willing to consider.

If you are having problems in your marriage, again, think of what you hope to achieve. Did your hopeful statement say, "I want a loving, harmonious marriage," or did it say, "I want a loving, harmonious marriage with my current spouse." This difference in how you state what you hope to get will lead to different possibilities to consider, and different research needed to understand more about these possibilities. With the first statement of hope, you may research into what it takes to have a loving, harmonious marriage. But you may also research into divorce, since that may be a possibility to you. In the second case, you would not research about divorce since you want to focus on your current spouse.

Net, it is really important to determine what outcome you hope to achieve correctly, because it will shape what you are open to consider and the specific information you need to gather about it.

You may have noticed a pattern here. In the first step, you research into the outcome you hope to get. In the second step, you gather information on the possible solutions you are considering to get that outcome. You want to find out the key advantages and disadvantages of each of the possible options.

It sounds quite simple but there are a couple of things to keep in mind. The first is a bias with respect to the possible options. You may think your marriage is beyond repair and a divorce is the best option. When you are in a state of emotional turmoil, getting out of a marriage might seem like you are being rescued from hell. But if you collect information with a bias toward divorce as being the best option to pursue, you will miss some of the problems that come with a divorce.

In fact, I want to bring up a major stumbling block that almost everyone encounters when they set out to find answers to touchy questions. The problem is our own bias and the fact that even the most even keeled person has some built in bias. So we tend to look for information that confirms our beliefs.

Confirmation Bias

When we begin to seek information that would help us make better choices, the first problem we encounter is confirmation bias. Wikipedia has this to say about confirmation bias:

Confirmation bias, also called **myside bias**, is the tendency to search for, interpret, or recall information in a way that confirms one's beliefs or hypotheses. It is a type of cognitive bias and a systematic error of inductive reasoning. People display this bias when they gather or remember information selectively, or when they interpret it in a biased way. The effect is stronger for emotionally charged issues and for deeply entrenched beliefs. People also tend to interpret ambiguous evidence as supporting their existing position.

Ralph Waldo Emerson summarized this concept in much simpler terms, "People only see what they are prepared to see." As we discussed previously, you must be open to seeing things from a different perspective. If you are not open to seeing things differently, you are operating from a confirmation bias. Your efforts to make informed choices will be stymied.

It would be nice if we could just give up our preconceived ideas and beliefs. Of course, that is not possible. We can't just start over with a blank slate. When we are faced with making choices, we bring all our past experiences with us.

But if we wish to make better choices, we need to be adequately informed about the possible choices and the consequences of each of them.

So how might a person guard against confirmation bias? To illustrate, let me give you two highly controversial topics – the death penalty and abortion. Now I am not advocating a position on either topic. But if you are like most people, you hold rather strong views about both these topics. Are there any possible circumstances when you might consider exceptions to your strongly held beliefs? If you are unwilling to even entertain the idea of some conceivable exceptions, then you have a strong case of confirmation bias. You are only going to consider arguments that support your point of view. To counteract confirmation bias, you must be willing to actively search and investigate positions that are opposed to your point of view.

This is going to be a difficult pill for most people to take. But you really need to seek out and consider opposing views. I am not suggesting that you need to adopt an opposing view, just see if you can find any possible value in a position contrary to the one you currently hold.

You may also consider seeking out some authority figure that holds a different opinion than you do. Then listen carefully to the basis for their position. Do not listen with the intent of countering each argument. Listen for understanding.

I am certainly hoping that when you seek to make better, informed decisions, you are not working on such controversial topics. But the best way for you to counter confirmation bias is to deal with some tough subjects. Then when you are dealing with less difficult topics, it will be much easier to handle.

To recap, you want to collect information on the outcome you hope to achieve and also on the options you are willing to consider for how to get from where you are to where you want to be. And in looking at the options, you want to make sure to be as unbiased as possible so you don't unfairly lean to one option versus another.

No matter what situation you are facing, someone has previously experienced a nearly identical situation. Look for people who have faced your situation and wrote about their experience. You can generally gain some valuable insights from someone who has actually walked on a similar path.

2) HOW TO COLLECT INFORMATION

At one time in history, information was a valuable resource. Those who controlled information were powerful. There is an old saying, "Knowledge is power." I am not sure that saying is as relevant any longer. It seems that information is becoming more democratic – that is, most people have easy access to a vast amount of information.

With so much information available, where should you start looking in order to become adequately informed?

I think it helps to be clear about your challenge before you jump into the search. Here is what you need to consider under the "How." You need to find, collect, sort and manage the information relative to the topic at hand.

So just where to you start and how do you find and collect the information?

Here are a few steps to help.

1) Step one is to write out all the possible options as precisely as you can.

The clearer you can be on a possibility you want to consider, the better.

2) Step Two is to then make a list of authoritative sources where you can collect information.

You can certainly start with the obvious – a search engine like Google, Wikipedia, Amazon.com (for books on the subject), and YouTube for audio/videos on the subject. Those are all public sources of information, and are great for a first round of general information. These sites might give you an overview or point you toward more specific sites.

There are literally thousands of Internet websites that feature some very valuable content and for the most part, it is totally free.

When you type in what you hope to accomplish, you will see a plethora of information about the subject. Let's take some examples.

If we continue with the topic of career and you went to Google and put "career change" in the search box, the first three search engine returns would be ads from companies trying to sell you something. At the time I did the search, the next listing was an article from Forbes magazine, "16 Things to Think About When You Are Considering a Career Change". The next listing was an article from Monster.com, the employment advertising service, "10 Worst Career – Change Mistakes". Both of these articles could give you some important things to consider as you make your list of possible options and how to achieve them.

If you are having difficulties in your marriage and you typed "marriage advice from a divorced woman" into the search engine, you would find a series of articles giving the pros and cons of getting a divorce. An excellent place to start collecting information.

3)   Step 3 is to tailor even more.

For purposes of illustration, I started with very general terms. The more specific you are, the more the information will be tailored to your situation. So instead of "career advice" you could enter "changing career at 50" or whatever terms better describes your situation. The more specific to your situation, the better the results will match your needs.

4)   Learn from experts and trusted authorities

After you have collected information from some general sources, you may want to consider some more specific information from some experts.

TED talks and its offshoot TEDx are a collection of talks by some of the most recognized authorities from around the world. The TED (Technology, Entertainment and Design) talks are videos from the TED talk conferences. Most of the talks are around 20 minutes or less and are some of the most informative and enlightening talks you will find anywhere. The website is **www.TED.com**.

If you go to TED.com and type "career advice" in the search box, you will find several talks from some very successful people and recognized experts in that field. These talks will often provide insights and alternate perspectives. They will certainly give you some ideas on additional avenues to explore.

Likewise, the Aspen Ideas Festival is an academic convention held each year in Aspen, Colorado. The cost to attend the festival is several thousand dollars. But the organization has put all the talks by the various lecturers online for free. These talks generally feature the most recognized professors from their various fields. You can search the talks by year, topic or speaker. The discussions cover a wide range of topics. The website is: **www.aspenideas.org**.

Let me go on a tangent a bit here to share something I think is key. A common theme in many of our hardest choices is what to do to improve our lives.

A lot of our disappointments in life occur when our expectations and reality do not match. So it can be beneficial to have a good understanding of realistic expectations about life. If our expectations are well grounded, then our reality will closer match, and we will not experience wide gaps.

I say all this because I think there are two presentations on the Aspen Ideas website that are helpful in providing better insights into understanding what leads to a more meaningful life. One is by Dr. Dan Gilbert, a Harvard University psychologist, titled *Stumbling on Happiness* (he wrote a book by the same title). Here is a link to the talk: **http://www.aspenideas.org/session/stumbling-happiness**.

The other is by Professor Jonathan Haidt, titled *The Psychology of Happiness*. Here is a link to his talk: **http://www.aspenideas.org/session/psychology-happiness**.

Everyone knows that Google is the largest search engine around. And you have probably heard of some of the great things they do for their employees. One thing you may not have heard about is Google Talks. This is a feature where Google invites well-known and highly respected authors/authorities on various subjects to give lectures at Google headquarters. You can find some very interesting and highly informative subjects covered in Google Talks. Search at: **www.Google.com/talks**.

Amazon.com is now the largest seller of books. One of the really nice features of Amazon.com is the ability to search for books by various topics, to find similar books, to search the table of contents of most books and to find insightful reviews of many books. In your search for information, do not overlook Amazon.com. If you really need to dig deep into a particular question, a good book will often provide a wealth of information. Check the table of contents, read the various reviews and make sure that the book is exactly what you need before investing the time and money reading it.

If your search for information is very specific and you find all these general sources do not satisfy your needs, then I have one additional recommendation. You can go to www.Allexperts.com and search for an expert on the particular question you have. The site offers specific answers from experts in various fields. You can search for experts by topics and by sub-topics. Then you will find a list of experts under each specific topic. You can review the biographical information about the expert and their feedback ratings. You will direct your question to a specific expert. You have the option for your question to remain private – just between you and the expert. The expert will not have access to your personal email address or any other personal information you choose not to provide. So you in effect get to ask an expert, get a reply to your specific question and still remain anonymous. You also have the opportunity to ask follow-up questions. The service is totally free.

Pick any subject and you can find an enormous amount of information available on the Internet. But there are some questions that are specific to you and your individual circumstances that cannot be answered by the general information you find. In those instances, you will need to narrow your search for information.

For instance, if you are having relationship issues with your spouse/partner, you may find lots of helpful information about how to have a better relationship. But you may still be at a loss for what to do in your particular situation. You want information – and often advice – to meet your specific needs.

Do you talk with your trusted friend? They may know you and your partner, but do they have the professional training necessary to help you? You could talk with a member of the clergy and seek counsel. But are they properly trained in relationship counseling to give you the information you need?

3) VALIDATING INFORMATION

This brings us to the subject of validating information. When faced with a problem, we often turn to close friends and relatives for guidance. Our close friends and relatives may sincerely want to help but their knowledge may not be sufficient to do so. Their perspective is probably biased. You must be careful when relying on information from friends and relatives. It may not be objectively valid.

We also could seek the advice of a professional. If the issue is medical, legal or psychological, there are plenty of professionals we could seek out for help. But unless we have some way to vet their qualifications, we may be led astray. Just because a person has a professional designation is no guarantee that their advice will be of value. References from those they already helped are a great way to validate in this situation.

Separately, we talked about getting information on the Internet. The value and veracity of what is there can vary widely. Many people claim to know the truth or be "the expert." It is your job to find out how much of an expert they really are. So, as you collect information from various sources, it is good to be a little skeptical about the value of the information. Because of the Internet, we are now blessed with an unlimited amount of information. But unfortunately there is no single authority that can vouch for all of it. So as you are evaluating the validity of the information you are collecting, be sure to ask yourself a few questions:

1) How do I test this information?

2) How do I know this information is trustworthy?

3) What is the motive of the source of this information?

4) Are they trying to sell me something? What is their agenda?

5) What are the credentials of the source of information?

Be careful that you do not fall victim to some persuasive arguments that are designed to influence you to take some action that is not in your best interest. I've seen lots of these "helpful" information sites that give half-truths in an effort to further their own economic agenda.

In collecting information about your problem, you may find some sources that are directly contradictory to some of the other sources you are using. Then you will need to study the qualifications of the various sources. If your question involves politics, religion, diet, or health issues, it is more difficult to find a consensus than contradiction. In those cases, where many so-called "authorities" disagree, you will need to do some research and study to find what is most helpful. Be careful that you do not allow your confirmation bias to influence what expert you choose to follow.

As you start to sort through the information you have gathered, an important question you need to ask about each piece of information is: Is this true? Keep in mind that very few things in life are absolute. Most things are neither black or white – but some shade of grey. But the more you can gather factual data versus opinion, the more valid it will be.

4) HOW MUCH INFORMATION IS ENOUGH?

When collecting information, it can be tricky to know when you have collected enough. You certainly do not want to fall into the trap of continuously collecting information and never making a decision. On the other hand, it would be a mistake to cut off the search before you had collected sufficient information.

Keep in mind that when dealing with complex, real time problems, we will never be able to collect all the information. There will be gaps. We will never have 100% of the information we would like to have in order to make a decision. But the truth is we do not need to have it all. As long as we have sufficient information, we will be able to make an informed judgment.

There are a few things you can do to test where you are on the collection continuum:

1) The first thing to do is to survey the information you have collected. Is the majority of the information heavily skewed toward a particular conclusion? If most of the information is leading you to a particular conclusion, you may need to take a devil's advocate approach and collect some information that supports an opposite view. So take a close look at the information you have collected. Are all the sources advocating the same position? If you collect information from 10 sources but the sources all say the same thing, you have not done adequate research. The purpose of collecting information is to be fully informed. This means collecting information that explores all sides. When you think you have done this, then enough is enough.

2) Another approach would be to find an acquaintance that might hold opposite views from you and try to sell them on your idea. Often an opposing view will bring out the weaknesses in your approach. If you find that

you cannot answer detailed questions or defend a position, then you probably need to collect some additional information.

There will always be more information out there, and we can't absorb it all. Use the 80/20% rule: if you think you captured *about* 80% of vital information about various possibilities, then you have done your job. Don't worry about the last 20% "out there." There will always be other sources we might have tapped, other sources we didn't even know about, other ways of getting information. Don't stress about the last 20%. When you've collected enough, it's time to move on.

Better informed leads to better conclusions.

Our goal in life is to improve our circumstances by making better choices. In the next chapter we will tackle the problem of analyzing the information we have collected.

We have seen that there are plenty of pitfalls that can derail our attempts to be better informed. We can fall victim to confirmation bias. We may fail to collect enough information or we may collect faulty information. We can also get stuck in trying to collect too much information – which can lead to putting off a decision because we feel the urge to collect more information.

So, here are the pitfalls to avoid:

1) Too little information

2) Too much information

3) Invalid, untrustworthy and/or biased information

The key is to get just enough objective information to feel confident that you can come to a conclusion as to what to do. And in the next chapter, we'll talk about just how to do that!

CHO**I**CE

INFORMED Exercise

You've decided what you **Consciously** want to change to get what you want out of life. You've approached the possible change with **Hopefulness** in mind. You were **Open** to possibilities. Now it's time to get **Informed**.

Here are a few questions:

1) Am I limiting my search to information that confirms my beliefs?

2) Am I trying to collect too much information? Too little information?

3) How do I know the information I collected is valid?

CHAPTER 8

CHOICE

C is for CONCLUSIVE

There comes a time to decide which path to follow - be true to your heart as you pick which to pursue

Conclusive:

1. Decisive, finalized, convergent

2. Able to end the debate

3. Definitive, involving a conclusion

4. Determined, resolute

5. Unwavering and firm

6. Strong-minded and willing to choose

Okay, let's be real. This is, by far, the hardest step yet for those of us who don't make decisions easily. It is much easier to possibility think, much easier to read articles and ask for opinions, much easier to...well, drag our feet...than it is to be conclusive on one option and let the others go. Call it what you will – fear of commitment, fear of loss of other opportunities, fear of making the wrong choice, fear of being a laughing stock, fear of missing out, fear of - well, you name it. We have a lot of reasons why we put this off. And yet, all the work you have done so far will, in effect, be wasted if you cannot take this next crucial step.

So, gulp… take a deep breath. It is now time to be conclusive and decide on a course of action.

So first, pat yourself on the back. You have done a lot of work so far. You started by becoming **Consciously** aware of what you really wanted to change in life. You were **Hopeful** about the outcome, and you were **Open** to looking at possibilities, even from a different perspective. In addition, you did the research, becoming **Informed** about the possible choices. So, "ready or not," you really are ready.

But, before we go into the different approaches of how to be conclusive, I want to warn you about a few traps that keep us from coming to good conclusions. Even if we have good information, we can fall into these traps. Think of them as holes in the ground – we don't want to fall into them so we need to watch out for them.

Trap 1: Thinking there are only two choices.

In most cases there are more choices than we acknowledge. Let's make it specific. Say you are unhappy with your job and you have another job offer. You may think that your choices are limited to staying with the current job or taking the new offer. One offers you security, but the other has more excitement. But is it possible to stay at the same company and do different kinds of work? Is it possible to get the security AND excitement? Has this even been explored? Don't conclude too fast between possibilities if there may be another good one (or even more) on the table. It is often not as black and white as we make it out to be.

Trap 2: Electing not to be conclusive since none of the choices are easy

Not being conclusive is giving up control. It is being reactive, allowing the circumstances to control your life instead of being proactive and taking control of your choices and therefore your circumstances. Be conscious of the times you are giving up the opportunity to exercise control over your circumstances by not being conclusive.

Because if you choose to do nothing, you have basically concluded you'll just go with the status quo. And how much is that going to move you towards what you want out of life? Instead of moving forward, you may just stay stuck in repeatable patterns, repeatable outcomes, same old, same old. Taking no risk, but in reality, risking your happiness because you are not making progress.

Trap 3: Not uncovering the "Hidden Payoffs" of a Choice – aka, being hijacked by subconscious needs

You would think some choices are easy. Or at least seem easy when there is overwhelming information that it is the right conclusion. The choice to give up smoking, for example. There is undeniable proof – tons of great, proven information - that it is hazardous to your health. So, what's holding some people back from stopping? Yes, it is addictive, but people quit all the time. And yet others continue to smoke. Why don't they just conclude it's bad for them and quit?

The payoffs of quitting are clear: 1) better health, 2) lack of harassment by people to quit, 3) saving money 4) clothes that don't smell, and even 5) not harming others through second hand smoke. But what about the benefits of NOT quitting? These payoffs often dictate our choice even though we don't like to admit them. In the case of smoking, these might be: 1) Feeling of autonomy, 2) Feeling of defiance to society, 3) Feeling that if we smoke we may not eat as much. We may just tell others that it's too hard to quit, but in truth, we don't WANT to quit because of the "hidden payoffs." Same goes for something like overeating and/or eating unhealthy foods – hidden payoffs may be that it 1) allows us to feel emotionally soothed and less stressed, 2) gives us something to do with our hands, 3) allows us to feel rewarded for putting up with the challenges of life, 4) makes us feel unrestricted and freer and/or 5) gives us a way to give ourselves the attention we may not be getting from others. Lots of emotional payoffs, but at what cost?

We need to examine these "hidden payoffs" and make sure we acknowledge them when making a decision. Because they can often hold us back or lead us to wrong conclusions if we don't uncover and deal with them.

Trap 4: Not thinking through Probable Consequences of a Choice

I remember one of the lines from Shakespeare's Macbeth when one of the characters is talking to one of the witches and says, "If you can look into the seeds of time, and say which grain will grow and which will not, speak then to me..."

Unfortunately, we cannot look into the seeds of time. We cannot predict the outcomes of our choices. But we can and should make educated projections. So when considering our Conclusions, we need to make our best guesses about the consequences of the planned actions. This is playing a "what if" game. What if I conclude to do this - what will happen?

Put yourself in the shoes of those who will be impacted by your decision. What do you PREDICT they might think, feel, do in response to your decision? Who might be affected? Who else? Think about all those who will be touched by your choice, and make sure to consider these potential consequences before coming to a conclusion.

Let's take a simple example. Even something like deciding to be healthier – this may impact what foods are in the house for your whole family to eat. Is it fair to the kids not to have any sweets in the house anymore just because you feel that having them there tempts you too much? Will they balk too much about this? If you think, "Probably so," then is there a way to make a more moderate decision that doesn't impact them as much? Is there a way to mitigate this - maybe allow them to eat sweets in their rooms? Maybe no sweets in the house but a weekend trip to Dairy Queen where they can have ice cream and you can just get a bottle of water?

So before making a decision, make sure to put on your "predictive hat" and guestimate what kind of impact your decision will have not only on yourself, but also on others. We can never fully predict what WILL happen, but we can often make good guesses at what might. Think through the consequences, and think about how to possibly mitigate any negative ones.

Trap 5: Falling prey to immediate gratification despite a long term cost

Whew – this is a big one! Humans are naturally biased to seek immediate gratification and to delay cost or unpleasant side effects. Said differently, we are more inclined to do things where the payoff is immediate and the "price we pay" is somewhere in the future. It is not enough to just think about the short-term consequences of your decisions. You also need to think of the long term ones as well.

This is a bit more complex than you might think. Some of our major problems stem from the timing impact of our decisions. Let me share an example. Consider education. When you consider education, there are two types of costs. One is the monetary cost and the other is opportunity cost. So you have the choice to get a college education or get a job and start earning money immediately. The cost, both monetary and opportunity, is immediate. You will need to pay for your tuition, books and living expenses as they are incurred. You will also incur some opportunity costs – while you are going to school and studying, there are lots of things you will need to give up. You will limit your ability to work, you will need to forego some leisure time and instead devote it to studying. So the cost is immediate.

The benefits, on the other hand, are somewhere off in the future. Statistics say you will probably earn more money as a college graduate, but that will be some four or more years in the future. You will probably qualify for higher paying jobs, career advancement and other benefits, but again, sometime in the future.

Our minds are hardwired to take care of today and to discount the future benefits. That is why dieting and exercising are so difficult to do. The cost is now and the benefits are somewhere off in the future. Everyone knows that a certain amount of exercise is good for your health and longevity. But what percent of people engage in regular exercise?

Realize that you will never have fortune-telling capacities. But that does not mean that you can't try to guess the long-term consequences. When seeking information about the timing difference, the first thing to do is just simply recognize our tendency to seek benefits today while deferring the cost of our actions. Healthy eating is the best example of this type of choice. Eating a large hot fudge sundae loaded with whipped cream can provide immediate pleasure. And we do not keel over with an immediate heart attack. In fact, for most people there is no immediate downside. But if we continue this sort of habit, we will eventually pay the price.

Another excellent example is credit card debt. Far too many people have huge credit card debt that they incurred as a direct result of immediate gratification while delaying the cost.

Along with recognizing the timing difference, the second thing we can do is to be honest with ourselves. We sometimes say, "oh, it's just this one time." Just this one time I'm overeating. Just this one time I'm yelling at my staff. Just this one time I'm doing this or that behavior that may have a long term cost. But is it? Or is it a pattern that's adding up to that cost? If it is truly an exception, then fine. Treat it as such, and then move on. But let's not kid ourselves if it's not. Let's not kid ourselves to think, "It is only this one time" when it happens all the time.

So, when it is time to be conclusive as to what to do, ask yourself if there is a timing difference between the cost and the benefit. Ask if you are taking the "easy way out" by reaping the benefits today, but costing yourself in the future. Ask yourself how much that cost grows by delaying it. And finally, ask how honest you are being with yourself. Your conclusion will always be worse unless you factor in the timing difference in the benefit and the cost.

How to come to a Conclusion

So how do you come to a conclusion as to what to do? Well, there are lots and lots of easy ways to do this. You could flip a coin. Consult a Ouija board. Pick petals off a daisy alternating the options. Paste the possibilities on a dartboard and throw the dart. Draw straws. Use a Magic 8 ball.

You could do any of these things. But I would not recommend it. When you make a choice based on chance, you are giving up control of your options. You are not using your noggin – or any of the information you collected to help you decide.

I don't know anyone who would resort to flipping a coin for an important decision. We want to believe we exercise control over the important choices in our lives. But at times that is not true. We already talked about the trap we could fall into of allowing things to happen rather than making a decisive choice. When we have trouble coming to a conclusion as to what to do, we might put off making the decision. This can result in an outcome decided much like flipping a coin! So here are some better ways of arriving at a conclusion as to what option may be best for you.

Let's take a look at these one by one.

Rating

One of the easiest ways to look at possibilities is just to rate them. On a scale of 1-10, given the information you've collected, how much do you like this possibility? Now go onto the next possibility, and rate that one. And so on.

You could also choose to rate it on a particular attribute. For instance, you might decide you want to rate it on how much you think it'll make you happier. Or how much you could fit it into your life. Or how much you think it connects with your goal. Or how much you believe it'll impact others. Or any other attribute that you believe is vital to your conclusion.

Often, a rating can give you a good first cut at what possibilities to keep or eliminate. If something is rated below a certain number (and you can determine this number), you can take it off the table. Just based on what you know about it already and your gut reaction. Sometimes this alone brings you the option that you want to pursue – you pick the one you rated the highest. Or sometimes it narrows your possibilities, and then for those that stay on the table, you can do some further analysis.

Cost Benefit Analysis

One of the best approaches you can use to converge on a decision is to do a cost/benefit analysis. The simplest form of a cost benefit analysis is to take a sheet of paper, draw a line down the middle and list the benefits (advantages/pros) on one side and the cost (disadvantages/cons) on the other.

You've collected a lot of information and the cost/benefit analysis is a way to start sorting it. And one great way is to put it in a pro/con list.

I have done this exercise hundreds of times – from simple questions about where to take a vacation to some really life changing questions. In the simplest form, you list the pluses and minuses of an option. In this simple format, the advantages and disadvantages are not assigned any degree of importance. The side with the most items listed generally carries the vote, simply because the pros *outnumber* the cons.

Weighted Cost Benefit Analysis

The simple cost benefit analysis is okay for choices that do not involve major life decisions. But if you were going to do a cost benefit analysis on some major life changing decision, you would want to take a more sophisticated approach. That simply means that all factors would not be given equal weight. You would need to assign some level of importance to each factor listed.

Let's look at a specific example. You are offered a new job at a substantial higher salary. But it requires you moving to a new location over 1,000 miles away. Here is what your simple analysis might look like:

Advantages	Disadvantages
Higher salary	Major relocation
Work in corporate HQ	Move away from established support
On fast track for executive level job	Uproot children from school
More cultural diversity	Higher crime rate
Better climate	Added stress of job
	Parents getting older, need help
	Must sell home in bad market

If you were doing a simple cost/benefit analysis, you might conclude that the disadvantages outweigh the advantages, simply because there are more of them. But if you were to give added weight to some of the advantages, for example, if the higher salary and being on the fast track for an executive level job are very important to this person, then the decision might swing in favor of taking the promotion.

One way to assign weight is to think of 100 chips that you could distribute. The more important something is to you, the more chips you can give it. But you only have 100. Where would you put your chips? Why? Using your chips starts to bring you to what you feel is *really* important in making your decision.

The weighted cost benefit analysis is a simple but effective method to evaluate the alternate choices and arrive at a conclusion. One thing you should guard against is the built in bias you may have for a particular choice. In the above example, you might be pre-disposed to seek the adventure of a promotion and the move. If you were, you would probably assign more chips to those pros that support your subconscious desire for a promotion and move. This doesn't mean you should redistribute your chips necessarily, but just be aware of your biases.

Reviewing Your Vision, Principles and Values

I'm putting this in the middle, but it is at the crux of coming to a conclusion. This is because it is often done in conjunction with other ways to make a decision – especially when those ways still seem insufficient on their own to guide our conclusions. Vision, Principles and Values are often needed to guide us toward the REALLY tough decisions. The ones that don't have clear answers no matter how many consequences we consider. We need to search our hearts to come up with what is right for us.

So how do we do this? First, go back to feeling Hopeful. What did you envision? Can you close your eyes and see that vision in your head? What is it telling you about which option to pursue, now that you have more information? What feelings does it evoke that could guide you?

Next, think about what principles you hold, as well as your values. Principles are key beliefs we have that shape our thinking. For instance, July Garland said this about "Being Yourself: "It is better to be a first rate version of yourself than a second rate version of someone else." Do you agree with this principle? Does it help you in making a decision? What other principles do you hold? Here are a few more examples of principles that I personally hold dear:

➤ **Humility** will earn you more respect, admiration, and recognition than having a big ego ever will. If you are really good at what you do, it will show through what you accomplish.

➤ **Ability** depends on the time and dedication you spend honing your craft, often building on innate talents

➤ **Abundance** surrounds us. If we approach life thinking there are always lots of other opportunities and paths - versus limited ones - we will better create and find them.

➤ **Confidence** comes from knowing yourself. It cannot be bought, and it is not dependent on how many material objects you own.

➤ **Vengeance** never solves a problem. It is always better to go with the path of love and forgiveness, not the path of fear, hate or force.

➤ **Nastiness** is learned, not innate. The nastiest of people are those who are most unhappy with their lives, and need someone to support and love them and lift them up.

➤ **Beauty** comes in all shapes, sizes, ages, genders, forms, races, and colors. It is important to embrace the beauty that is you, versus try to conform to a "society viewpoint" of it.

It is important to think about the principles that you hold to see how they guide your decision making. Jack Canfield and Janet Switzer wrote a wonderful book called *The Success Principles*. Their premise is that the more of these principles we hold, the more successful we can become, and the more we can use them to guide our decisions.

And how about values? What do you value most in life? Your belief in God? Family time? Helping the environment? Helping other people? Again, let these guide you to a conclusion.

There was a time when my daughter had a difficult decision to make between two great summer internship opportunities. One would have given her experience at a firm that makes a lot of hygiene products. It would have given her exposure to top management, a great paycheck, and the ability to live at home and save money over the summer. The other paid a lot less, but gave her the opportunity to do research on stress and anxiety. It was a tough, agonizing choice, and she asked me to help her think through it. I had her list out the pros and cons, and even weigh them. But there was no clear-cut answer because both had some really great advantages, and some disadvantages. In the end however, she valued doing research on the human mind – and helping out humanity this way – more than she valued helping humanity by making a better hygiene product. She valued the fulfillment she thought she'd get from the brain research more than the paycheck/savings and industry experience she'd get from the hygiene product research. She also followed her principle of abundance – thinking there will always be other industry opportunities out there should she decide to try one later in life. Once she made her decision, she happily sighed with pride and relief, having followed her values and her heart.

This is an example how there is no "right or wrong" conclusion – only the conclusion that a particular path is "right or wrong" for you. Other people would have snapped at the industry opportunity in a heartbeat, and may even think she was wrong not to have taken it. But who cares? She felt great because she let her values and her heart decide. And that made it the right conclusion for *her*. That made it a better choice for her, which is all that mattered.

Asking for Help

You will need to live with the consequences of the path you choose, and you are responsible for the consequences of your choice. But that does not mean that you necessarily need to make the decision all by yourself. There are occasions when the best conclusion will be reached by asking for help.

The key to this tactic is to be highly selective in who you ask for help. It is very easy to seek help from those you feel most comfortable asking. This might be a co-worker, a relative or a close friend. Chances are the first person that comes to mind will be "safe," that is, you will feel comfortable asking them and probably believe that they think along the same lines as you do.

It is probably not very helpful to ask someone whose thoughts mirror yours – someone who will validate your opinion but will not challenge you to look at things differently.

It is also not very helpful to ask someone to be "the answer man (or woman)" and decide *for* you. Your goal is not to transfer the decision to someone else. The ideal person to ask for help would be someone who will help you think through the alternatives and the consequences of each one. You have more information about yourself than anyone else in the world. So the ideal person will not provide you an answer, but rather, they will help you discover the answer you already have inside you.

When seeking out such a person, look for someone with a few scars. People who have not experienced some ups and downs in life will not have a good perspective. As Benjamin Franklin said, "After crosses and losses, men become humbler and wiser." You want to ask someone who has experienced some "crosses and losses." They will not be as certain of the right answer but will be more open to helping you look at the possible choices, explore the alternatives and think through the consequences.

There are a couple of additional qualities you should look for in your advisor. First, they need to be a good listener. You want someone that will allow you to tell your story. A person who wants to jump to the bottom line is not really going to be helpful. Secondly, they should not be judgmental. When a listener starts judging what you have done or what you should do, they are shifting the conversation from being about you and your choice to about them and their values/beliefs. This will not result in a good decision for you. If you feel like you are not being heard, your best course of action would be to cut the session short and seek another advisor.

As I mentioned above, my daughter sought my advice about which summer job to take. My goal was not to make a decision for her but to help her sort through the pros and cons of the opportunities, clarify her values and principles, and arrive at the best decision based on those. Asking for help can be a powerful way to arrive at the best solution. The process of having someone listen to your story and possible solutions will often provide you insights that you would never get without going through the process.

The other way to "ask for help" is ask what you *think* a trusted advisor, friend, mentor, parent or someone else you believe has your best interest at heart would tell you to do. Sometimes merely just thinking about this helps. I have seen the bumper stickers that say "WWJD?" which stands for "What Would Jesus Do?" The people in that car probably seek the love and trust they have in Jesus for guidance on their decisions. Likewise, you could use others in this way. Perhaps your mentor passed away, but you could think about what he or she might have told you to do in a certain situation, to help shape your conclusion as to what to do. You "ask for their help" in your mind, and think about how they would guide you.

Group Decisions

We have been talking about arriving at a decision based on something you want to achieve. We have talked about ways to individually come to a conclusion. But there are many times when your choice will have an impact on others. If you are in a committed relationship, the decision to change jobs or relocate needs to involve your significant partner and perhaps other family members. Project at work? Often you need to decide with others. Some decisions need to be made by more than one person. You may have gone through all the CHOICE steps so far on your own or you may have already involved others in them, but now that you have come to the Conclusive step, it is vital to involve others who will be impacted as part of the decision making process.

Rather than refer to the other members by a variety of different names/titles, I will simply call them stakeholders. They will be impacted by the decision – they have a stake in the outcome. All stakeholders may not have an equal share in the outcome. But they all have a vested interest in the outcome so it is important to consider the various points of view and ensure that the interest of the group is aligned.

Before you can engage the other stakeholders in the decision making process, you will need to share all the steps you have gone through to this point if they have not yet been involved. Asking them to help make a decision without taking them through each step is going to result in a poor decision.

Group decisions can involve a wide range of situations. Work, family, friends, and recreational groups are some examples. The level of emotional intensity will vary depending on the group. The more intense the emotional relationship, the more time and effort you will need to spend on sharing the information you developed to the current point.

Once all the members of the group are comfortable with the process, it is time to decide on how to proceed to a decision. Here are some ways to proceed:

1) **Voting** - You could arrive at a decision by a simple majority vote. Everyone gets one vote.

2) **Weighted voting, Type I** - You can assign stakeholders different voting power. The stakeholders with the most at stake get more say in the matter. Or the stakeholders who are higher up get more power. An example of this is that maybe the boss gets three votes while everyone else on the team gets one. Or that the parents' opinions count more than the kids' – even though the impact of a decision may be on all.

3) **Weighted voting, Type 2** – In this way, everyone gets three votes, but they can use them however they see fit. They can put one vote on three different options, or if they really feel strongly about a certain option, they can

use all their votes for that. This helps show the strength of people's feelings toward one option or another.

4) **Negotiation and Consensus** - Another possible arrangement – one that takes the longest, but yields the most support - would be for the group members to debate the various options and arrive at a negotiated solution they can all back. For example, if you are considering a new job that would require relocation, the various stakeholders (relationship partner and any children) might offer up compromise solutions that you might not have considered. They might also share concerns or perspectives that you had failed to include in your original set of options. So in this case you might be able to arrive at a consensus conclusion from a collaborative effort. Consensus means you have the *consent* of all the participants. It doesn't mean that it is the "favorite" solution of everyone, just that it is agreed to and supported by everyone. Negotiation helps build consensus because it shows you are taking others' needs into account. With group decision-making, the more the possibilities can be discussed, and consensus reached, the better the support for follow-through.

Decision Tree

Another method to help you arrive at a Conclusive choice is a decision tree. You see these used most often in business settings, but they work equally well with individual or group issues outside of business.

The technique is named a decision tree because the decision can have many branches and the major branches can have smaller paths that branch off the larger one. They often help us think through consequences and secondary decisions (and beyond) that will need to be made based on the key decision.

Basically the decision tree starts at one point, generally depicted on the left and as you move to the right there are alternative paths (branches) and each decision will result in an answer that will further move you along the path. A decision tree has you make decisions at every step of the way, and begin to think of consequences of every step to help you sort through which path to go down.

Here's an example. Let's say you were seeking a new job/career and you had two offers – Job A or Job B. Job A might require you to relocate to a different city. So you start going down that path. Relocating to a different city might involve two or three communities near the major city where Job A would be headquartered. So then you move down the path of selecting one of the communities, keeping in mind you want a suitable school district for your children. Selecting a school would then influence where you might look for a house to purchase.

On the other branch – Job B might mean that you were shifting careers. Shifting careers could involve additional education/training. There might be two or three options for getting the additional training. Getting the training may mean a shift in schedule in order to care for your school age children. It might also mean that the lower earning spouse might have to reconsider their work situation and goals.

A decision tree can have as many branches as you want – it all depends on how much you want to "think out" the consequences. Or decision trees can help you think out the reasons of why to pick one choice over another. On the next page is a simple example of a decision tree, showing the reasons that the decision maker is giving for the various options on the tree.

This decision tree is about where to go on a vacation:

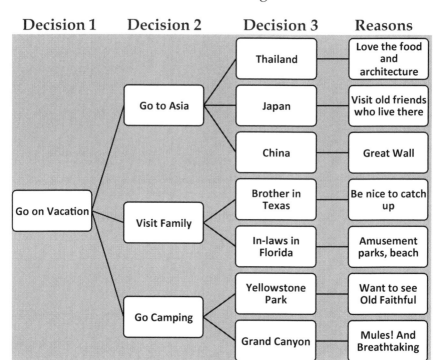

| Decision 1 | Decision 2 | Decision 3 | Reasons |

In this example, the first decision is actually whether to go on vacation or not. This chart assumes the answer is yes, but another chart may have that as a question mark and lead you down other branches of the tree if the answer is no (maybe you delay and save money for next year, for instance). The second decision in this tree leads you to three different types of vacations, and the third one leads you to different options within each one. Finally, in this example, some of the reasons are predicted for each of the possible alternatives.

When faced with complex decisions, it is often necessary to map out the options, the alternative paths and the consequences and/or reasons of each choice. This is a very simple explanation of the decision tree. Most college level business programs have an entire class devoted to this concept. There are many books available which explore the technique in great detail. The purpose here is to give a brief introduction to decision trees and when it is appropriate to use them.

If You Have Tried Everything, and Still can't come to a Conclusion

There will be times when you are stuck. Really, deep in the mud and can't get out of it. You looked at pros and cons, you did a decision tree, you asked for help, and you looked at your values and principles. And yet, you are still stuck and can't conclude what to do.

So here's one more technique for moving forward. It is best explained by using an example. Let's call it "The Choice Has Been Made" technique. With this, you need to envision life as if "The Choice Has Been Made" already, and the other choices are off the table. Completely off the table. No going back.

Let's look at an example.

Say you are in a job you find unpleasant and have been offered another position but you have doubts if you would actually improve your situation by taking the new position. Find a quiet place and relax. Try to eliminate all distractions. Now focus on the choices. Then pick one. In this case, let's say you decide to quit your job and take the new position. Tell yourself that you've made up your mind, you are leaving your current employment and taking the new job. Let that thought totally sink in. Accept it. Envision it. Then notice how you feel. Did a feeling of calmness come over you? Or are you really feeling stressed out? If you make a decision and then measure how you feel about it, your gut reaction will generally let you know if the decision was correct. If you get the jitters, you probably made the wrong choice.

"The Choice Has Been Made" is a powerful way of recognizing where your heart really is. It is key to really believe the other choices are off the table when you do this to get a true read on your feelings. We can often gain insightful information by testing ourselves this way before we actually announce our decision to others. It is a way to tune into our gut, our instincts, and our own sense of what's right for us.

When You Fear Your Conclusion Might still be Wrong

If you really fear this, well, don't worry – you haven't acted on anything yet. But ask yourself why you fear this. Do you think you weren't adequately informed? Well, there's usually still time to gather more information. Do you feel that there is no way to *ever* be adequately informed? Well, we can only do our best to guess at consequences given the information at hand.

Remember, hard decisions are by their very definition not made easily. So they often come with questioning ourselves. Just realize that life is a gamble. We all at times make choices that turn out not to be the best. Sometimes we don't anticipate consequences well enough, but other times situations change and affect us.

One way to mitigate possible negative consequences is to create a contingency plan. That is, have a plan for what to do just in case your choice leads to results you did not anticipate. A back-up plan, if you will. Think ahead that if your decision doesn't lead to the results you want, there is another way to get there. Businesses use contingency plans all the time – for instance, if they rely on a vendor to source a material, and the vendor doesn't come through, they whip out their contingency plan to see how else they can source it. It's not a bad idea to think, "If this doesn't work, then my backup plan is this." But don't let it sidestep you from doing everything possible to make your initial plan work.

Also, sometimes we just can't predict the future enough to know if a contingency plan is needed. For instance, I know a person who took a new job in New York on September 5, 2001. He moved his family there, and was excited to start this new venture. Less than a week later, terrorists killed over 3000 people and the city was in shock. His new job located near the Twin Towers was put on hold. Did he make the wrong decision to go to New York? Of course not. He could have never predicted what would happen. Did he create a contingency plan in case a terrorist attacked? Again, it never occurred to him to do so because the attack was so unexpected. He didn't say, "Here's my contingency plan just in case of a terrorist attack." No one would have expected him to do this. Instead, he had to quickly determine how to make adjustments so he could earn an income while waiting for his new job to be available again.

The key to conquering your fear about making the "wrong" choice is to know that in life, we can always make adjustments. We are not stuck forever going down one path. If it hurts others, you can apologize and amend. If it hurts you, then learn from it and move on. The key is not to stick with the choice that is not working (because perhaps you feel ashamed to admit you made a "mistake"), but to learn, grow, and develop from it. And make another conclusion that better serves you and those affected.

Action Planning:

Now that you have reached a conclusion, it is time for the final step, and that is to put together your action plan. Action Plans bring our conclusions to life. Once we decide what path to take, the action plan paints the steps along the path.

The Action Plan can be as simple as a to do list, with steps to be taken and when they need to get done. If your decision involves other people, and they are part of your plan as well, write down who does what and when. And often it is key to include *how* the steps will be taken.

Some people keep their Action Plans in their heads, and that's okay, but often it is useful to write down what you are going to do, and by when. It is a helpful way to make sure you are staying on track and moving forward.

In the business world it is critical to do this – businesses use action plans all the time, for both individuals and groups, as a way to ensure alignment, accountability and tracking. But even for other decisions in life, it is useful to write down what you now concluded to do, and break it down to what, when, and how!

CHOI**C**E

CONCLUSIVE Exercise

You've decided where you **Consciously** want to change to get what you want in life. You've approached the possible change with **Hopefulness** in mind. You were **Open** to possibilities. You became **Informed** about various options. And now it's time to be **Conclusive** as to what to do.

So answer these questions:

1) What methods will you use to make your conclusion?

2) Using these methods, what's your conclusion as to what to do?

3) What is your Action Plan to bring what you've concluded to do to life?

CHAPTER 9

CHOIC**E**

E is for EXECUTED

Decisions are pointless unless they are executed. A choice without action is as useless as no choice at all

Executed:

1. Performed, done, carried out

2. Fulfilled the command or purpose of

3. Delivered, completed

4. Acted upon to deliver the result

5. Acknowledged and pursued

6. Brought to pass, accomplished, achieved

Don't worry – there will be nobody killed in this chapter. Isn't it funny that we have hijacked the word "execute" to connote something deadly? We think of executions - beheadings, lethal injections, mafia hits, sniper shots, and all kinds of other ways people are put to death. And while "deprive of life" is certainly one definition of the word, there is so much more that the word "execute" means. There is a whole range of positive connotations. When we execute something, we perform it. We deliver it. We pursue it. We fulfill it. In other words, we DO it. We act on our decisions. Our plans get carried out. Our words become our actions. And our actions lead us toward the change we want. A CHOICE is *never* complete until it is executed.

Ready, Aim, Aim, Re-Aim, Aim again...

Let's think about this with a simple story. Four guys were going skydiving. One decided to jump. How many skydivers were left in the plane? Simple math, right? Did you say three? Well, not so fast. One decided to jump, but did I say he actually DID jump? He may have decided but then backed out when he saw how far down it was. He may have gotten scared to take the plunge, thinking he might land in the wrong spot. He may have wanted to jump, but only if someone else went first. He may have decided and gotten a last minute call from his wife pleading him not to do it. There is a huge difference between making the decision to do something and then actually doing it.

Let's look at something that a lot of us do – make New Year's resolutions. Come January, you'll see lots of advertisements to join gyms and weight management programs for those of us who've decided to become healthier. You'll see storage containers promoted at stores for those of us who've decided to get more organized. You'll see a surge in dating site advertisements looking to attract those of us who've decided this is the year to go out and find the perfect mate. And sure, some people act on these resolutions (at least for a while). Others, on the other hand, just make empty promises to themselves and take no action.

Likewise, with our endless lists of things to do. How many do we actually do? Maybe some, but other things remain undone. Maybe these things need to go on a "not to do" list versus a "to do" list! Or perhaps a "just to think about" list. Let's call it what it actually is. Seriously, if we don't plan to actually do it, then get it off the "to do" list.

Teddy Roosevelt had a great quote: "In any moment of decision the best thing to do is the right thing, the next best thing is the wrong thing, and the worst thing you can do is nothing." Now, you may be thinking that it is better to do nothing than the wrong thing. But is it? Don't we learn from our mistakes? Don't we live life by not only glorifying in our successes, but by strengthening from our failures? I often tell people if everything is going perfect for them, they are not stretching themselves enough. We need to move beyond our comfort zones, and yes, that will indeed make us uncomfortable. But it will also make us feel alive. It will give us new opportunities, open new doors, and move us beyond the intellectual exercise of deciding what to do and into the action of doing it. We will live life, warts and all, not just think about it.

Nike says, "Just Do it." Do you have to be a star athlete to "do" it? Of course not. In fact, most of the things we do, someone else has already done or can do better. So what? Who cares? We often get frozen in our tracks because we feel too vulnerable to take action. We feel afraid of the risk. What if it doesn't work out? What if I'm rejected? What if the action leads to something bad? What will people think of me? How will I feel about myself? How will I explain? How can I do something that might embarrass me? Or even hurt me? What if it sets me back? How, how, how can I take action without a 100% guarantee of success? And so we plan, and plan, and re-plan to avoid doing. We avoid doing because maybe right around the corner there is another decision that's better. Maybe if we just aim more, we will be more precise. Maybe if we just aim, no one can hold us accountable for doing anything wrong. We can relax and just laze and do nothing. What's wrong with that? We avoid stress that way, right?

There is an old Yiddish proverb that says, "Man plans and God laughs." We cannot guarantee success of anything in life, because life is filled with uncertainty, complexity and volatility. We make decisions, and act on them, based on our best guess of what will lead to a certain outcome and based on seeking information and thinking through consequences. We take steps to minimize our risks. We choose options that we think will work out best. But we are not seers that can see into the future. We don't know if the consequences we predict are the ones that will happen. We do not even know if all the information we base our decisions on is perfect (think of the Iraq war - no weapons of mass destruction hidden after all). Face it - we just don't know what we don't know.

So given all this uncertainty, maybe it is just best to avoid action. Maybe that will help us avoid stress and worry. Maybe it will keep us from biting our nails. And yet, our inaction actually brings on a different kind of stress. We end up kicking ourselves – why didn't I go after that new job? That pretty woman? That healthier version of me? That bigger role at work? That opportunity to speak to a group? When we do nothing, we constantly think of what might have been, could have been, or would have been. We regret and belittle ourselves for not trying. We fear hanging our heads from failure so much that we don't realize that doing nothing actually makes us hang our heads more. Net, we feel worse about ourselves when we take no action! When we take action, and it doesn't work out, we can say, "Well, at least I tried." We can give ourselves credit for taking action, even if we end up needing to adjust our plans and decisions. But inaction often leads to more self-doubt and feelings of unworthiness. It leads to stagnation, depression and beating ourselves up for not taking steps towards a positive change.

So action is not only worthwhile, it is the very essence of living, growing, and feeling empowered.

Let's think about it as if you were building a house. You research for the right location with good school districts. You look at models with different floor plans. You search stores and the Internet looking at appliances. You find out what permits and inspections you need. You think about the use of the space, and what furniture and fixtures are needed. You look at flooring, paint colors, moldings, and other decorative details. After all this work and all this research, and decisions you make about all these elements, would you then stop? Would you plan, plan, plan, and then not build? Barring an emergency (dropped all your money in the ocean?), of course not. You would go ahead and build your house. And yet we decide where we want to change, research our options, and even come to conclusions, and then don't go the last step of executing against our plans. We stop short of taking action. We put the brakes on when we actually have to DO something. We come up with great ideas, plans, and intentions, and yet don't act on them.

As we've discussed CHOICE so far, we have talked about consciously deciding where to change. Being hopeful about it. Being open to different options. Seeking information and thinking through consequences. And then being conclusive on what to do. But the rubber is now ready to hit the road. You have now become ready and you've aimed. It's time to take the last step. It's time to build the house. It's time to fire. Otherwise, it just becomes "Ready, aim, aim, aim, aim, aim…" No action = no fire.

Hmmmm - now I've planted firing squads in your mind. No wonder it's so difficult to execute. We think of it as so – well, so final. Once we take action, we've *really* committed. Once we actually start executing our plan, we're "out there." We become more vulnerable because now people can see our flaws or mistakes or missteps. Yikes!

Dr. Brene Brown is a leading researcher and expert on vulnerability. One of her quotes on it is: "Vulnerability is the birthplace of everything we are hungry for." We want to make this change, but know by executing – by taking steps to make it – there is a good chance we will sometimes stumble. And we feel vulnerable about it. Dr. Brown also says, "Sometimes the bravest and most important thing you can do is just show up."

Eddie Rickenbacker, a WWI aviator, said it this way, "I can give you a six-word formula for success: Think things through – then follow through." Simple, sweet, practical, and oh, so scary sometimes. Which brings us to the land of excuses.

How Big is your "But?"

Once when I presented a workshop on this book to a group of women, they laughed because they thought I was asking them, "How big is your butt?" Perhaps we should just talk about getting off your butt! There are so many reasons we procrastinate in executing our decisions. We could go deep into our psyches and determine why we aren't moving forward and taking action. But here are seven top excuses that often come up.

1. **The "Too Yucky" Excuse**: "This action will just be too painful, boring, expensive, complicated (or other fill in the blank bad adjective)."

2. **The "Too Busy" Excuse**: "I have too many things going on and just can't add this to my plate."

3. **The "Too Uninformed" Excuse**: "I just need to read a bit more, learn a bit more, think it through a bit more, and compare a bit more before I act. Yes, I know I

sought information and even concluded what to do, but gosh, what if I missed something?"

4. **The "Too Worried about what Others May Think" Excuse**: "If I do this, and don't succeed, what will others think? How will I stand it if they judge me to be imperfect? I don't think I can stand the embarrassment or shame I'll feel."

5. **The "Too Early to Act" Excuse**: "This really doesn't need to be done until later, so why bother starting now? What's the harm in waiting until closer to when I really need to do something?"

6. **The "Too Unimportant" Excuse**: "I thought this was important to do, but maybe it's not, so I'll let it sit."

7. **The "Too Stressed" Excuse**: "I just think doing this will add to my stress level, and I'm so stressed already, so better to just not do it then."

Do any of these excuses sound familiar to you? Which ones do you use the most? Some of us tend to use one type of excuse more than others, while some of us are more situational in the way we use excuses. In this situation, I'll use this excuse. In that situation, that excuse. So let me ask you - how big is your "but" that's keeping you from getting off your butt?

Nolan Bushnell, founder of Atari Computer said, "The critical ingredient is getting off your butt and doing something. It's as simple as that. A lot of people have ideas, but there are few who decide to do something about them now. Not tomorrow. Not next week. But today."

What are you doing *today* to take action towards the change you want to accomplish to get what you want in life? And to get rid of your "but?" What can you do <u>right now</u> to carry out the first part of whatever you're avoiding? I'm not saying you need to carry out your whole plan in a day –

Rome wasn't built in a day – but what can you do to *just get started?*

To help you, let's look at those excuses again, and this time focus on counter arguments.

1. **The "Too Yucky" Excuse**: "This action will just be too painful, boring, expensive, complicated (or other fill in the blank bad adjective)."

    Think about: What's the opportunity cost of NOT doing this? How painful will it be if you don't move forward? How Yucky is the current status quo?

2. **The "Too Busy" Excuse**: "I have too many things going on and just can't add this to my plate."

    Think about: What can be dropped that's less important? If this change is needed, isn't it worth making the time to do?

3. **The "Too Uninformed" Excuse**: "I just need to read a bit more, learn a bit more, think it through a bit more, and compare a bit more before I act. Because what if I missed something?"

    Think about: You've done your homework. You've looked at alternatives. There will always be more out there to know, but you can never know everything. Don't try to.

4. **The "Too Worried about what Others May Think" Excuse**: "If I do this, and don't succeed, what will others think? How will I stand it if they judge me to be imperfect? I don't think I can stand the embarrassment or shame I'll feel."

    Think about: The people who matter most in your life will support you even if you make a mistake or stumble a bit. They understand we are all human. The people who don't know you that well, and who may judge you more harshly - well, really, who cares what they think? Don't give them that kind of power over you to stop you from taking action. As Taylor Swift sings, "The Haters gonna hate, hate, hate, so shake it off, shake it off!"

5. **The "Too Early to Act" Excuse**: "This really doesn't need to be done until later, so why bother starting now? What's the harm in waiting until closer to when I really need to do something?"

    Think about: Some of us like to do things only when under pressure, but then we run the risk of running out of time or not completing what we want to do. Are you one of those people? Why do that to your self? Start now, and pace yourself so you can breathe easier.

6. **The "Too Unimportant" Excuse**: "I thought this was important to do, but maybe it's not, so I'll let it sit."

    Think about: What changed to make this not important anymore? Did it really change, or are you just looking for a way out? Go back and really question your motives, and ask yourself: If I don't make progress in this area, will I care? Will I kick myself? Often the answer is yes since it really is still important.

7. **The "Too Stressed" Excuse**: "I just think doing this will add to my stress level, and I'm so stressed already, so it's better to just not do it then."

    Think about: What kind of stress will you feel by *not* making progress in this area? You went through all the steps to decide to do this – from consciously choosing to change all the way to concluding how to - chances are you'll just stress out more by not following through on the promises to yourself.

We plan so we know what to do, but then we have trouble actually doing what we planned. If change were easy, we wouldn't struggle with it so much. We wouldn't come up with excuses not to do it. It is easier to think about becoming healthier, but much harder to actually eat better. Easier to think about starting a new career, but much scarier to do when we get a steady paycheck now. Easier to surf dating websites looking for that perfect person, but much harder to be vulnerable by sending someone a message to say hello. Easier to say we'll focus on our family more, but much harder to find the time to do it. Change is much easier said and planned than actually done.

Little Itty Bitty Baby Steps

But guess what? There is a key to making change easier. There is a secret to actually executing your plans, not just intellectualizing them. And that is to act like a baby.

Okay, not totally like a baby. I don't want you to cry out your excuses. That would be ineffective. But I do want you to act like a baby learning to walk.

If you have ever seen a baby learning to walk, they are excited. They want to do it. They're tired of just crawling to get around. They know they can make a positive change if they just learn to stand on two feet. And take a step. Okay, maybe they're wobbly at first. Maybe they fall the first few times. Maybe it takes days or weeks to get steady. But they keep trying. They stumble, and get up and try again. And again. And eventually, after taking little baby steps, they're walking. Then running! Weeeeeee! Freedom! Progress! New adventures ahead!

Getting what you want in life takes action. It takes executing your CHOICE. But it doesn't have to be heroically large action. In fact, we are usually more effective when we take baby steps. What ONE thing can you do TODAY to move you toward your goal? What one thing can you do tomorrow? What about the next day? Week? Month?

If you start lifting weights, you are not going to start with weights that are way too heavy for you. You start with small weights and work yourself up to heavier ones. If you start too large, you are bound to put yourself in harm's way.

The key to executing your CHOICE – to realizing the change you want to make – is daily effort. Wake up, focus on what you want, and do something toward it. Wake up the next day, focus on your goal, and do something toward it. That doesn't mean every day will be perfect. It doesn't mean that there won't be days that you fall down like the baby trying to walk. It doesn't even mean there won't be days when you fall backwards. You will. All of us do. Life is filled with imperfect tries. Maybe on that day, you just reward yourself for attempting to take that step. And you just try again the next day.

Or maybe one day, you lose your focus, and give up. Okay, do it just that day. Tell yourself that the next day, you're back on plan. If you continue to focus on making progress toward what you want out of life, and you do it mindfully every day, or even most days, you *will* reach your goal. If you see yourself wandering away more than a day, bring yourself back and begin again. Execute against your plan again. Steadily take the baby steps. Just continue to return to the goal, return to the goal, return to the goal. Use it as a mantra. Chart your progress and then self-correct. Use information you learn along the way and charter a slightly new course toward your goal.

And let's understand one other thing about babies. When they fall, they do not criticize themselves. They do not say, "Oh, I can't believe I did that!" So, again, I want you to act like a baby. Stand up, dust off, try again, and move on. If you take time out to criticize yourself, versus asking, "What can I learn from this?" you are just wasting valuable time, energy and focus. It will only distract you and discourage you. Instead, just refocus on the goal. Refocus on the end you want to achieve. Baby steps. Baby steps. Baby steps. They are the key to success.

With this final step of "execute," we've come to the end of the process. The Power of CHOICE is now yours. Go get what you want out of life with it!

CHOICE

EXECUTED Exercise

You've decided where you **Consciously** want to change. You've approached the possible change with **Hopefulness** in mind. You were **Open** to possibilities. You became **Informed** about various options. And you were **Conclusive** as to what to do.

So - time to **Execute**!! But first, a few questions:

1) What excuses are you using to not take action to get what you want? How can you counter these?

2) What is the pain of not taking action?

3) What Baby Step can you take today? Tomorrow? The next day?

PART 3:

Examples & Frequently Asked Questions

CHAPTER 10
CHOICE Examples

So how does all this work in REAL life?

This chapter contains eight short, simplistic examples of some common choices people need to make and how this method helps. It is not exhaustive – there are SO many choices that people need to make all the time on how to improve their lives, but it will give you a running start. Some of these may apply to you, while others will not. The key is to get this process in your head so it becomes a natural part of your decision-making. If you go through all the steps, you will actively transform your life.

We'll cover examples on careers, teamwork, marriage, dating, parenting a child, fitness, aging parents, and debt management. These examples are taken from real life, with some details changed to protect identities.

The short format of these is to give you a quick start. I could write a whole book (and books have been written) on each of these topics, so this does not pretend to cover these thoroughly. And the details of your own situation certainly will not exactly match any of these – we all have unique circumstances. What your particular problem is, what you hope to achieve, what options you are open to consider, what you need to know about them, what you conclude to do and even how you go about executing against your plan – these are all highly dependent on you.

So let's get those juices flowing by showing you some common examples on how you can use **The Power of CHOICE!**

EXAMPLE 1: Career Conundrum

Carla is at the end of her rope. She has been passed over for a promotion twice, and just feels burnt out with her job as a resorts sales manager. She doesn't even like sales, but it helps pay the rent. She comes home every night tired and frustrated. Her husband is getting the brunt of her bad moods, and is asking her if it's time for a change. Something has to be done before she goes crazy and makes him crazy too.

C = Conscious

Carla is aware that she needs a career change. She makes the conscious decision to find a career that is more satisfying.

H = Hopeful

"I wake up every morning excited to go to work because I love my job so much."

O = Open

Carla starts thinking about her likes. She would like a job where she could be more creative. She also wants to feel more in control of her own destiny. She'd like to make a bit more money. Her preference would be to work with others she finds interesting. She thinks she'd enjoy writing and speaking. She'd like to build off her past experience rather than start something completely new. She wants to feel worthy and respected. And finally, she'd like to help others learn. What kinds of jobs might be possible to meet these all these "likes?"

Carla paradoxically brainstorms jobs she'd hate to do: being a construction worker, being a research assistant, answering help calls all day, cooking at a restaurant (she does NOT like to cook!), and other jobs she would absolutely despise. And she looks at the list and decides what she dislikes about these jobs – and then uses that to build her "like" list. For instance, she would dislike working in a lab all day since she likes to interact with other people a lot. She would dislike answering help calls because she can't sit still very well. She realizes she really likes to move around when she works. She dislikes construction work because she doesn't like heavy tools, but she *does* like building on ideas! And so on.... She starts opening her mind to different possibilities.

Carla then goes to see a career counselor and talks to him about what she likes. He gives her some additional assessment tools to open up her mind further to different possibilities she might want to consider as she changes careers. She reads the book *Cool Careers for Dummies* to further think of possible careers she might like.

I = Informed

Carla seeks out information about some of the possibilities that most interest her. Are there any job openings in her area? She gets on job websites such as monster.com, indeed.com, and careerbuilder.com. She asks friends, family and neighbors if they know of any openings. She gets data about the salary range of different possibilities. She takes a course in resume writing to become better educated on how to position herself. She talks to people in the fields she's considering to see what they like most about it and to understand if it really is a good fit for her. She also talks to them to find out more about how she can get a similar type of job.

C = Conclusive

After seeking out information about possible jobs, Carla decides to use a weighted pro/con list. The weighted pros tell her that the ideal job for her would be in corporate training and development. She gets to help others. Be out of her seat while training. Write curriculum. Speak. She can build off her past experience as a sales manager, and teach about influencing customers, but she knows she's not limited to that topic. Through her research she found that corporate trainers often teach all kinds of performance related subjects. She's excited to seek a position in this new field. She's excited to do something she thinks she'll really love.

E = Executed

Carla sends out resumes and gets some interviews set up. She builds sample curriculum to share with recruiters. She hates all the rejection letters and feels like giving up, but doesn't. Instead she learns from them, tweaks her resume, sharpens her interview skills, and goes out and tries again and again until offered a job. It doesn't pay quite as much as she wanted, but still better than what she made previously. She's thrilled to start her new career. Once she gets her offer, she goes and hands in her resignation at her old job. She's feeling on cloud nine.

EXAMPLE 2: Marriage Mayhem

Jerry is screaming at Mary Beth again. He's angry that she didn't pick up his dry cleaning like he asked her to do. He seems to be constantly yelling at her for one thing or another these days. And he's been calling her names as well, saying things like "I can't believe you're so stupid." This is not the loving, considerate man she thought she married. He's become disrespectful and unkind. And often he's uncommunicative. He walks away and doesn't bother to answer her. She could yell and yell and yell, and he just ignores her. Which makes her yell even more. Why can't he talk to her? She asked him what's wrong, and he says he's just tired, but she suspects it's something else. She thinks he's tired - of her. He has been staying out and "working late." Mary Beth thinks he's having an affair, but doesn't know for sure. And, of course, he won't admit anything to her. She asks him if he still loves her, and he says, "Stop acting so needy, I love you, alright?" She doesn't know if those are just empty words, especially since he gets in a dig first and says it so snidely.

She also realizes that they've been getting into a lot more power struggles lately. Fights over how things should be done, who does them, what's right, and what's wrong. It seems if Mary Beth says white, Jerry says black. The old "if you loved me you'd do this" countered with "if you loved me, you'd never ask me to do this." Mary Beth just doesn't know where or how this will all end. She married 'for better or worse,' but the worse is just running the show right now.

She does know, however, that the yelling and disrespect are making her life miserable. She feels so disconnected from her husband that she's contemplating a divorce. But she's not a quitter, and she's very worried about how their kids, ages 5 and 8, will cope. She cries most days about it and feels helpless. How did her marriage become such a wreck?

C = Conscious

Mary Beth realizes she can't go on in such a discordant marriage. It is not fair to her or the kids, or even her husband, to live life with so much stress all the time. She has always placed a high priority on her marriage, but she knows the difficulties that lie ahead. She either needs to fix the marriage or get out of it. She decides she ideally wants to repair it. If she can't, and if her husband is totally checked out and not receptive, then and only then will she contemplate getting a divorce.

H = Hopeful

"My marriage to Jerry is harmonious and joyful. I give love and support and I feel loved and supported."

O = Open

Mary Beth starts thinking about options to make her marriage better. She knows that marriage counseling needs to be considered, but she's not sure Jerry will go. But she lists it (never rule out anything in this step). She also thinks going by herself to a psychologist is an option. And she has heard of marriage coaches – people who aren't psychologists but have helped couples, so she puts that on the list as well. There are lots of books on marriage, so it's an option to do it the self-help way. She can join a woman's support group and see how others cope with their marital issues. She can also look at marriage blogs and forums for advice. She can talk with friends who seem to have successful marriages (no one really knows what goes on behind closed doors), and ask them for tips. She can call on some of her husband's friends and tell them she wants to surprise him with a great day out – asking them what he might like – to try to rev up the marriage. She can make a conscious effort to just be nicer, more attentive and more loving, in the hopes he will be as well. Maybe she can ask about his day more, and just listen. Maybe she can show more appreciation versus judging him so much. Or perhaps she can start gently touching him more…giving him a shoulder rub, touching his cheek, hugging him from behind. It would be totally different from what she does now. Would it work to make their marriage better? She put it on the list as a possibility.

I = Informed

Mary Beth talks to some friends and family for advice, and particularly takes notes from ones who have great marriages (how do you keep it so great?). But she is also interested in learning from those who had marital problems but saved their marriages. What did you do to repair it?

She asks her husband if he would consider counseling, and he adamantly says no. She doesn't push it at this point since she doesn't want another power struggle. She talks to a few counselors who have good reputations, to see if there is one she might like to use, even by herself.

She starts looking at marriage forums online, and finds she is really not alone in her struggles. So many people have similar issues. She finds some comfort in this, and also learns what others have done to help their marriages.

She starts reading a lot of self-help books, and finds out that she can open the door to positive connections and nurture her partner more. That she can escape the destructive patterns that have been playing out over and over again in their marriage. She reads about negative relationship dynamics and sees herself and her husband ("Oh my gosh – this describes us exactly!"). She takes quizzes to better understand the personality clashes that they've been having. She learns about different ways to communicate – ones that are helpful and not harmful – and how to talk about a problem without fighting about it. She learns about triggers, and understands better what to say and what not to say when conflicts arise. She learns how to become a better listener and partner.

C = Conclusive

Mary Beth examines her values and principles in the midst of her marriage mess. Her values tell her family comes first, and she uses this to fight the feeling to just "give it all up." She decides that she needs to focus on the principle of reciprocity. She will become more loving, and hopefully this will trigger her husband to be more loving as well. Mary Beth decides she needs to go to a psychologist to help her, because she knows, at least right now, she unilaterally needs to put forth effort to save the marriage. She decides on one that helped her friend's marriage.

She thinks about all the advice in the self-help books and forums, and starts to conclude which behavior modifications would work best in her particular case.

She decides to talk to her husband's best friend as well, just to ask him for a get-away idea. She wants a special date with her husband...time to start having some fun again.

E = Executed

Mary Beth calls the psychologist and makes an appointment. She calls her husband's best friend, and although at first he's reluctant (maybe he thought she was going to ask him to intercede?), he is fine with giving her an idea for a date that Jerry would like. He suggests she surprise him with tickets to the Mets baseball game coming up. She goes out and buys them and gives them to Jerry. He says, "What's this for?" She just replies, "Because I care."

Mary Beth starts to use her newfound skills and knowledge to change in little ways. She asks Jerry more about his day. She doesn't let "the small stuff" bother her so much. She is careful not to escalate arguments. She asks him more about himself, and she complains less. She points out what she likes about him, and is more attentive and less judgmental. She approaches issues with a problem solving hat on her head, not with an accusation hat on it. She is calmer, more nurturing, more forgiving to her husband as well as to herself.

At first, her husband doesn't seem to notice these changes. But then one day he calls her by the old nickname he had for her, "sweetums." Her heart is fluttering. Could he be feeling more affection for her again? She thinks so. And likewise, she is feeling more for him. He is not screaming as much, and when he does, she uses her skills to de-escalate it faster. They are now problem solving together, and they seem to enjoy each other more. Mary Beth knows it will take time, but the healing has definitely begun.

EXAMPLE 3: Team Tension

Richard hates going to his weekly product launch team meeting. Everyone on his team is polite, but you could virtually feel the undercurrent of tension. No one wants to step on anyone else's toes, or expose them selves, so people are reluctant to share. This has resulted in a series of bad decisions, project stagnation, and finger pointing. The department heads have begun to get nervous that the planned launch will be delayed, or worse, fail altogether.

C = Conscious

Richard knows he needs to get his team, and the project, back on track. He meets with it and mentions that he thinks their dynamics will continue to derail them. He makes them all consciously aware that it cannot be "business as usual" anymore, because "business as usual" is not working. Most of the team members agree that an improvement is needed, starting with agreeing on what they hope to achieve. They all write their own version of what they want, discuss it, and then they agree on the following statement:

H = Hopeful

"Our team enjoys working with each other and are doing what is needed for a successful product launch."

O = Open

Now, the hard part. How to do it? Richard knows he needs to improve the teamwork and it cannot be done overnight. But he also feels uncomfortable taking too much time off to team build versus do real work. However, using the human resource department (HR) as a partner, he starts to open up to the idea that team building *is* real work – because it will improve the effectiveness and efficiency of the team. He also opens up to the possibility of getting rid of a team member if he needs to end up doing so to make the team more cohesive – although only as a last resort. He considers various ways to mend the team – asking HR what can be done internally, but also looking at external team building options. Several of the options offer team functionality assessments and/or behavioral assessments and then dedicated time to tackle the issues. While other companies offer more fun social activities to do. Hey, might be fun to go camping together! With all the companies offering different programs, he asks HR, management, peers and even friends what they have used so he can be sure to put various options on his list. He wants to be open to different possibilities that might work for his team.

I = Informed

Richard asks the companies to share their recommended processes for building his team. He learns about the costs and time involved in the various options he is considering. He works with his management and team to delve into the budget and see what they can reasonably afford. He also looks at testimonials and asks for references to see how effective outside vendors are. Additionally, he asks the vendors if any of them specialize in product launch teams, as this may sway him. He also wants to know how much they can customize their programs to fit his needs. Finally, Richard learns from a peer that used an internal resource from HR for team building that there is a risk of losing objectivity. He told Richard that the HR person who facilitated his peer's team seemed to have a bias toward one of the team members he worked with in the past. This was his opinion, at least. His peer recommended an outside facilitator for this reason.

C = Conclusive

Richard compares the various programs and decides he definitely doesn't want a "fun" team building one. While these may increase team camaraderie, he doesn't think they go far enough to solve deep-seated problems. He also eliminates the option to have an internal HR facilitator, based on his peer's warning. Looking at the processes, pricing, and time involved in the outside programs, he decides to go with one that can customize to his needs. He also likes the programs that assess both the dysfunction of the team and the different styles of its members, as he believes this will give them a better plan to improve the team. Finally, he considers the actual person from the company who would be his facilitator – he liked one person in particular's easy-going style. He thinks this will be important since the team currently has so much tension. Richard works with his team and the outside facilitator to plan out a one-and-a-half-day team building offsite, including pre-work for it, as well as follow-up meetings.

E = Executed

All team members take the team functionality and behavioral profile assessments before the offsite. At the offsite, they review the assessments, and do various exercises to build trust, become better at conflict management, and increase individual commitment and accountability to team goals. They then meet a week after the offsite to review their commitments and any issues they feel are still outstanding. In their regular meetings, they are purposeful in referring back to learning from the offsite, and as conflict arises, they use new learned skills to manage it effectively. Because they build up more trust with each other, they are more willing to share ideas and feedback, without fear of repercussion. It seems team members are now laughing more in meetings and even teasing each other a bit more. The team gets approval from management to adjustthe timing for the launch by three weeks, but for the most part, gets back on track.

EXAMPLE 4: Dating Dilemma

Andy is not finding the right woman. Everyone he meets seems to be self-involved or just not into him. He is sick of the bar scene, sick of online dating, and sick of his mom asking him if he's met anyone. Maybe he should just live life as a bachelor.

C = Conscious

Andy is aware that he really does want to find a special woman in his life. He makes the conscious decision to continue to seek her out.

H = Hopeful

"There is a great gal out there just waiting to meet me."

O = Open

Andy asks himself "What kind of woman would I be open to? Have I been limiting myself too much in my requirements of her? Why, why, why?" He starts looking at how he judged women in the past. He seems to have ruled out some for rather inane reasons like "Oh, she wears too many earrings in her left ear" or "Oh, I can't date her because she's eight months older than me." Why did these things matter? He realized that there really are maybe only a handful of musts in a great woman for him: a little silly, smart, thoughtful, loving, stable, someone who shares his values - things more related to character and intelligence. And yes, someone he is physically attracted to so there is enough chemistry. But she doesn't have to look like Cameron Diaz - just someone with nice eyes and a sweet smile. With a much smaller requirement list, possibilities open up.

Then Andy thinks about whether he had been limiting his exposure to meeting people. Where else might he go? He says to him self, "If I did know where to look for that special woman, where would I look?" "If I did know where nice gals hang out, where would that be?" Maybe at a church fundraiser? Maybe at a library or hospital doing volunteer work? Maybe on a more targeted website?

I = Informed

Andy asks a lot of his friends and family who are happily coupled where and how they found their partners, and what mattered most to them in who they picked. He researches for dating websites that might fit his needs better. He reads about local events and volunteer opportunities where he might meet someone with similar interests. He predicts that if he takes more time to go out to places that might have women with similar interests, he might have an increased chance of meeting someone he likes. Or he thinks a consequence of him joining might be that someone at one of those events may have a woman they'd like him to meet. Maybe even someone saying, "Oh, Andy, you're so sweet – I told my niece all about you and she said you sounded nice. Can I give you her number?" He found out one of his friends met his wife this way, so, hey, it's possible, right?

C = Conclusive

Andy uses a decision tree to sort through different ways to look for someone special. After laying it out and looking at it, he decides to join christiansingles.com to target his dating prospects better. He decides to join a soup kitchen to find others who like to help those in need. He also decides to join a yoga class because his friend met his wife at one. Finally, Andy also thinks about what he values more, and decides to focus more on a woman's heart than her hype.

E = Executed

He signs up for the new dating site, joins the soup kitchen, starts yoga (just to meet girls, but he actually kind of likes it now), and reprioritizes what he's looking for in the 'ideal' woman. He agrees to go on a blind date with a fellow soup kitchen volunteer's single sister. Well, he checks her out on Facebook first and thinks she's cute – no such thing as a real blind date anymore. They talk on the phone and she seems vivacious and sweet. He's excited about their upcoming date. Who knows where it will lead, but it's a start.

EXAMPLE 5: Parenting Problem

Twelve year-old Paul is sullen again. He sasses back at his parents and his grades are slipping. He doesn't seem to take interest in family movie time anymore, but just locks himself in his room after dinner. He gives one-word answers when asked a question, or screams, "I don't want to talk about it" or "Stop nagging me." He used to be such a happy little boy. His parents, Tom and Cindy, are concerned. They don't know what's causing Paul to be so mean, grouchy and disrespectful, and they don't know how to break through to him. They tried punishing him for sassing, but he still does. They tried asking him what the matter is, and he screams "Nothing!" They thought at first that this was regular teenage rebellion, but this has gone beyond normal angst. They know they have a very angry, unhappy child.

C = Conscious

Tom and Cindy decide they need to do whatever it takes to help their son feel happier and more engaged in life. They know they cannot let Paul fester any longer, and are committed to help him change for the better.

H = Hopeful

"Our son is doing well in school, has supportive friends, and enjoys family time. He copes well and is excited about life in general."

O = Open

Tom and Cindy first start to think about what might be causing Paul to be so mad and sullen. Is he being bullied? Is the work at school too hard? Was he rejected by a girl he liked? Did someone offer him drugs and he thought he needed to take them to be cool? Is he questioning his sexuality? Are we being too lax or too strict as parents, and it's causing him to be upset? They brainstorm possible troubles their son might be having, making sure not to rule anything out by saying "Oh, it can't be that...."

They put on their "Nothing is Have-To" mindset and start thinking about possibilities of their relationship with him right now. Do they have to nag him to try to find out answers? Do they have to punish him while he's already feeling down? Do they have to be his enemies? And they start thinking about possibilities that might help him. Does he have to go to the school he's going to now? Does he have to take the course load he's taking? Does he have to hang with the group of friends he currently has? Of course, they don't yet know the problem – so some of these possibilities may not make sense. Time to find out more.

I = Informed

Tom and Cindy make an appointment with Paul's school counselor. He is concerned as well, particularly about Paul's grades slipping. They ask him if he's seen anything at school, and he says no. He suggests Paul go to a psychologist and recommends a few. Tom and Cindy call them and seek information about their credentials and style. They call their insurance to see which ones are covered. Tom and Cindy also call friends and ask if they ever had similar problems with their kids. What did they do? They also visit their priest and seek his guidance. What does he recommend? Have other parish parents had these kinds of problems with any of their kids, and what did they do about it?

C = Conclusive

Cindy calls her mom to ask for help to sort through all the advice and information. The conversation leads Cindy to decide a psychologist is the way to go. She and Tom find a great one who has helped a lot of kids who are acting like her son. They decide that even though this person is not in their insurance plan, he is worth the investment because his reputation is so good. They value their son's mental health more than the money – they will cut corners if need be to do this. After listening to the priest, they also decide to be more sympathetic versus punishing to their son. Something is causing him to be very unhappy, and they don't need to add to that.

E = Executed

Tom and Cindy make an appointment with the psychologist and take their son for regular sessions. They act more supportive and encouraging to him versus yelling at him for not behaving. Through the help of the psychologist, and their new behavior, Paul opens up to them that he wet his pants accidentally at school when he laughed too hard, and has been the running joke ever since then. He has been called 'Peeing Paul' in the hallways. He didn't want to share this with his folks because he was too embarrassed and because he resented them for giving him a name that could be so easily ridiculed. Cindy, Tom and Paul work with the psychologist on what to do to help Paul cope better with the mean kids at school so he feels good about himself again and is more confident, collected, and empowered.

EXAMPLE 6: Forgetting Fitness

Brian is staring at his college pictures again – boy, was he fit back then! He could bench more than his body weight, and he had abs that every guy envied and every girl wanted. He looks down at his blubber belly now – too many beers, too much delicious home cooked lasagna, too little time to exercise with a job that gets him up at 5:30am and tires him out so much that when he gets home he just wants to relax. Maybe the belly isn't so bad – he's seen worse.

C = Conscious

A trip to the doctor tells him his belly *is* bad. The doctor is fearful that he's making himself a candidate for a heart attack. Brian decides it's time for a change. Maybe not the six pack abs of his youth, but a healthier weight so he's not a walking time bomb.

H = Hopeful

"I am healthy and fit."

O = Open

It's hard to think of possibilities to fit in exercise when his life is so regimented. So he starts by asking himself "If I did know when to fit exercise in my schedule, when would that be?" He considers 3-4 days a week maybe going in a half hour later to work so he can get in a quick workout. Or maybe doing something during his lunch break every other day. Or maybe doing something longer on the weekends and something at evening with the guys during the week. Then he asks, "If I did know what exercise would fit my busy lifestyle, what would that be?" He makes lists of things he used to enjoy but hasn't done in a while – biking, basketball, field hockey, and, yes, weightlifting. He also had some fun playing a little tennis, but never really took that seriously. And he knows a couple of his friends play racquetball, but he's never done that. He adds it to his list of possibilities though. And he lives near a beautiful park, so he decides to add walking and jogging as well.

Now, there's that other thing about fitness – the eating side. To Brian, the word "DIET" has always been a horrible four-letter word. He would joke that it starts with "DIE" as "I'd rather DIE" first. But now Brian realizes that's just what he might do if he doesn't start eating right. He starts listing all the things he likes about eating and drinking – the taste, the textures, something to do with his hands while watching TV, the feeling of family when they sit down for a meal together, the party hardy feeling when he's out with friends for a beer. He starts to think: Is it possible to do something else with his hands while watching TV, like maybe play Candy Crush? Could he still go out for drinks and drink only one light beer and the rest diet soda or, better yet, water? Is it possible to enjoy family time without second helpings? No one says you have to DIET to lose weight (nothing is a have to), but is it possible to modify just enough so he can feel healthier and still get in that great lasagna once in a while?

And finally he wonders if it is possible to eat better without counting calories, eliminating carbs or another food group, cleansing, craving, or any of the other things he usually associates with diets. He's hoping it is! He wants to be open to any eating plan that will still let him EAT and not worry every time something goes into his mouth.

I = Informed

Brian looks at his options and does some research. First, if he works out in the morning, he might want to bike, so he looks into the cost/types of stationary bikes. He also researches what local leagues are around for men around his age to play basketball and field hockey. He calls the tennis club and asks for rates and openings. He asks his friends about racquetball – what do they like about it, how hard is it to learn, is there a possible spot open if he decides to play, how much does it cost? He looks into buying a set of weights and a bench for home, but also calls a personal trainer to see how much he might cost, thinking that might be the best way to kick start him. He looks at gym membership as well.

On the eating side, Brian researches what others did to be healthier. He asks friends and family members who have recently lost weight and kept it off – and who now look a lot healthier - what they did. He also does a lot of research online as to weight management programs, and Googles "weight management" to find other ways to get a healthier body. He reads blogs from people who've changed their eating patterns and seem to be happy with their new habits. He also asks his wife what she thinks – what does she know or need to know about cooking a bit differently to support him in this goal to be healthier?

C = Conclusive

Brian rates his possibilities – on a scale of 1-10, what exercise does he like the most and of those things, he rates again - what's easiest to fit into his schedule? He decides to forego the gym (would take too much time to go) and instead exercise at home a few mornings a week. He decides he'll do both bike riding and weight lifting. He also decides that he'll join the racquetball group his friends have. Yep, he might look a bit foolish at first, but he'll learn. He figures that will be a fun way to get fitter.

As for eating, through his research he found the website "choosemyplate.gov" and decides to try it. It is absolutely free. And it will give him a better sense of control on what he's eating now and how to modify to eat better. He doesn't see tracking forever, but will do it just to get started on his healthier eating journey so he can begin forming better habits. Brian writes down an action plan when he's going to go shopping for equipment, when he's going to exercise, and when he's going to start using the website.

E = Executed

Brian buys a bike and puts it in his bedroom, where he can watch TV while riding. He starts riding three days a week for half an hour. He also buys a weight bench and some weights, and puts these in the basement where the family won't hear him grunting. He lifts weights one weekday and one weekend day. He buys a FITBIT to track his motion and make him more aware of the need to increase it. On days where he is not doing enough, he walks after dinner at the park. His wife joins him a lot, so that's nice as well.

Brian starts to ride his bike. He's doing well for a few weeks. Then he goes on vacation and it throws him off schedule. He doesn't ride his bike for a while after returning. But as his pounds start to increase, and his energy decreases, he starts over again. The key, he knows is to be *mostly* consistent and to get back on that horse if you fall off (or in his case, get back on that bike if you slack off).

Brian also goes on the choosemyplate.gov website and uses their tools to manage his eating better. He begins the eating modifications needed. His supportive wife even learns how to make lasagna that is delicious but a bit lower in calories. He is practicing a healthier lifestyle and is becoming more fit.

EXAMPLE 7: Senior Safety

Susan is worried about her mom, Agatha. She's been living alone in an apartment for over 15 years since Susan's dad died, but Agatha just isn't as "with it" anymore. She forgets things more easily, she isn't balancing her checkbook well, she loses track of dates and times, and isn't always clear when she speaks. Susan also suspects her mom isn't taking her medication correctly, as she has found pills on her floor. Agatha's driving is very shaky as well, and Susan thinks she should give it up. Agatha is resistant to do this, as she doesn't want to lose her independence. But Susan thinks she's putting herself and others in harm's way. She also thinks her mother should not cook anymore, as she left the gas on once accidentally and went to sleep. Thank goodness a neighbor smelled it in the hallway and they were able to clear the building. Susan is very concerned what to do with her mom to keep her safe. She also wants her to live out the rest of her life with as much joy and as little worry as possible.

C = Conscious

Susan knows it's time for a change before her mother harms herself. Status quo is just not working, despite her mom wanting to stay independent. She needs to spearhead this change since she is the child living closest to her mom, but she will also ask her sister, Rebecca, for help – especially when it gets down to concluding what to do. Rebecca agrees with Susan – something needs to change.

H = Hopeful

"Our mom is safe and happy."

O = Open

Susan wants to be respectful to her mom, so she starts possibility thinking by involving her. Mom, what kinds of things do you think might help keep you safe? Are you open to a lifeline pendant? To a helper coming in to cook for you and drive you to places? To a joint bank account where I can help you manage your money? What else might you be open to consider?

Her mom is a bit resistant to this conversation. It is so scary to admit she needs help. So Susan decides to lighten the mood and use paradoxical brainstorming. "Okay, mom, what can we do to make you UNSAFE?" Maybe hire a hit man to live with you? Have you burn a bunch of candles in every room, maybe even one near a breeze? Put stepladders everywhere and have you go up and down all day?" Her mom starts to laugh, and suggest more ridiculous ideas. "Maybe I can play with knives all the time? Maybe I can tell people on Facebook when I plan to be away so they can come rob me. Maybe I can give all my money to a 'Save the Spiders' campaign and then live in a homeless shelter." After laughing a bit, her mom is more open to seriously considering options. Susan is grateful that her mom can still be part of this conversation, since she has so many friends who have had to make the choice for their parents without their input since their parents were more incapacitated. They list out all kinds of possibilities: hiring a helper for a few hours a day, hiring a live-in helper, getting a lifeline pendant, moving to a continuing care retirement community, moving in with Susan or with Rebecca, moving to an assisted living facility, or maybe moving to a group senior home with a few other seniors.

I = Informed

To help make their decision, they decide to first visit Agatha's doctor. She recommends Agatha see a neurologist, who prescribes a brain MRI. The brain MRI shows there is cloudiness, which may have been caused by mini-strokes. The neurologist suggests they see a neuropsychologist and go through tests to better understand Agatha's mental capacity. Agatha takes tests at the neuropsychologist, and the results clearly show she is in the beginning stages of dementia. Agatha is heartbroken, but this piece of information helps her be more accepting that a change is, indeed, needed.

Susan does a lot of research on living options, first looking at in-home possibilities, and then looking at possibilities that would involve a move. She looks at what they offer, the distance from where she lives so she could still be close to her mom, the cost, the cleanliness, and most of all, the ability to keep her mom safe and happy. She talks to her mother about how important or non-important it might be to live with people of her own religion, since she is Jewish and her mother has always had mostly Jewish friends since she did a lot with her synagogue. She begins taking her mom to outreach programs offered by facilities (tea times, introductory sessions, a holiday meal), so her mom gets a better sense of what it might be like if she lived in a facility versus at her current home. To make her mom more comfortable with the possibility of moving, she even starts to call Assisted Living the "Senior Sorority House - with a few guys tossed in." She wants her mom to feel good about whatever decision is made that impacts where and how she lives.

Susan also has her mom talk to friends who have moved to facilities, and she talks to her own friends who had parents move to them. What did they like? What were their issues? What else should she take into account that she needs to know?

C = Conclusive

Susan calls her sister and they go through each option, and they think about the best outcome and the worst. They weigh the benefits, risks, and costs learned during information gathering. They give weight to those criteria that are more important to them, namely keeping their mother's safety paramount and their mother's happiness a close second. They put less weight on things like "needs to be a Jewish facility," since their mom said it's really not that important to her. They start to eliminate some options that don't seem to be superior – like keeping their mom where she is now.

Susan and her sister get on a conference call with their mom and ask her, "What do you think Dad – who is watching over us from 'above' - would like you to do? What in your heart of hearts do you think would really keep you safe, and let you live a relaxed life?"

After pouring over the options and information, Susan, her sister and their mother agree that Agatha would be safest and happiest in a senior living facility that could assist her in cooking, cleaning, and errand running. They pick one that has lots of activities to keep Agatha busy, some people that Agatha already met through outreach that she thinks might be good future friends, that is close to Susan, and is somewhat affordable (although they think Agatha might need Medicaid assistance at some point to continue to live there if and when her funds run out and she has greater health needs).

E = Executed

Agatha puts down a deposit to reserve a room. She gives the apartment complex a heads up that they will be moving once a room is available. Susan starts going through Agatha's things to see what she really wants to keep and what they can donate or discard. When the facility calls to say a room is available, Agatha is ready. Rebecca flies out to help, and they pack up their mom and help move her. After a couple weeks, Agatha adjusts and is now feeling at home in her new home!

Separately, Susan gets a Power of Attorney to help her mom with financial management and other matters relating to her welfare. She knows that as her mom gets older, her dementia will probably worsen, so she does this to be ready. Susan and Rebecca now feel relief that their mother is in a safe place and has even made new friends.

EXAMPLE 8: Debt Disaster

Sandy and Mike are deep in debt. When they got married eight years ago, they both had student loans, car payments, credit card debt from the wedding, and a lot of expenses associated with setting up a new home. They were already in a hole, but were making steady payments and trying to keep up. Three years ago, however, Sandy lost her job when her company laid off a lot of employees due to slow sales. She has been working as a temp while looking for full time work, but so far, no luck finding anything steady. Then two years ago, they had a child. It was a C-section, and Mike's insurance didn't pay for it all. Plus, the cost of diapers, formula, and other baby expenses all added up. The credit card bills kept getting bigger and bigger, and when they came close to maxing one out, they would open another card just to have more ability to spend. Now they owe over $41,000, and every day, with more expenses and more interest, it continues to build. They know they can't continue to rack up debt, but really don't know what alternatives they have. Instead of living the American dream, they feel like they are drowning in the American nightmare.

C = Conscious

Sandy and Mike realize they can't continue going deeper and deeper in debt. They were both counting on Sandy finding a new full time job sooner, but nothing is on the horizon. Time to face facts. Their expenses will continue to outweigh their income - unless they can determine a way to change.

H = Hopeful

"Our finances are solid. We have enough money to pay our expenses, save for retirement and college, and have a bit of fun."

O = Open

Sandy and Mike start thinking about this two ways – increasing income and decreasing costs. What might they do to increase income? Can Mary Beth work two or even three-part time jobs? Maybe something where she doesn't need to work a lot of additional hours, like selling cosmetics or jewelry online? Or maybe see if she can babysit for others while she watches her own little one? Or teach a Sunday school class? Or become a virtual assistant? Sandy starts giggling and says maybe she'll become a part time ballerina. This releases their stress and they come up with more ideas – maybe she could party plan or help people serve when they throw parties. Maybe she can become a senior companion a few hours a week, and take senior citizens errand running. Maybe she can become a Weight Watchers coach, since she went through their program and was successful. All of a sudden, a lot of possibilities start to appear. She could still look for that higher paying full time job with benefits, but in the meantime, there does seem to be ways to get a bit more money.

And how about Mike? Can he ask for a raise or find a job that pays better? Maybe it's time to freshen up his resume and look around as well. Maybe he can even consider something part time himself – mowing lawns on the weekend? Taking a night job? Maybe HE can be the virtual assistant!

And while possibility thinking, they also think of any ways to ease some of their debt quicker. What about any relatives who might consider gifting them some money now versus bequeathing it when they pass away? Or maybe a garage sale, with neighbors donating their "junk" that they don't need so they have lots of items to sell?

And then there's the cost savings side. Where can they cut down? Is it possible that Sandy can manicure her own nails? Is it possible Mike can make coffee and have a bagel at home versus buy them every day at work? Can they find perfectly good (but gently used) clothes for themselves and their baby at second hand shops? They make a list of 'little expenses' that are niceties versus necessities. And then they think of bigger expenses. Do they need to live where they live, or can they downsize? Can they sell either of their cars and buy a lower cost one?

And what about the cost of credit? Is it possible to transfer balances to lower interest rate cards or even ask their creditors to lower their rates? Can they get a consolidation loan to make payments more manageable and to get rid of their highest interest rates? Should they consult with a credit counseling agency for tips? Maybe they can call their student loan creditors and see if they can forgive any of their debt. Is it worth considering bankruptcy?

I = Informed

They decide to start by getting a complete picture of their debt. They gather their most recent statements for their credit cards and loans. They get a credit report and their credit score to see where they stand. They make a list of all debts – creditors, interest rates, balances, and what their minimum monthly payments are. With it all laid out on one page, they can eye where to target adjustments (like, get rid of the highest rate cards). They open a free account with Credit.com to see what kind of low rate balance transfer credit cards they can get. They go to a credit agency and are given advice on how to consolidate.

Sandy starts searching for another job. She looks online for opportunities as well as asks friends. She finds out that some things – like becoming a virtual assistant – may be tougher than others. There would be more set-up work required in starting her own business. She asks friends and family for advice, and they tell her to go for something as flexible as possible. They tell her she's really good at helping people, and it's nice to learn that's how people think of her. Sandy calls Home Care agencies, and she also calls Weight Watchers to find out more details about opportunities they may have. She also calls her church to ask about Sunday school needs. They tell her that they don't have a need for a Sunday school teacher, but inform her there is a preschool teacher opportunity at an affiliated place. Huh! Something she didn't even consider!

Mike asks for a raise and is told it will be considered, but not right away. He starts looking at other opportunities in his field. He looks online, and checks with friends and family. He also calls the local Chamber of Commerce to see if they have any leads. In the meantime, he also looks for some part time work that he could do. It's hard to find, but after a lot of research online and talking to people, he finds a restaurant looking for an extra valet on Friday and Saturday nights. The local hardware store is also hiring. He always *did* like playing with tools.

C = Conclusive

Sandy looks over the types of opportunities and the pros and cons of each. She puts a lot of weight on flexibility since she wants to continue taking temp office jobs. She thinks that being a weight management coach will give her the most flexibility, and an added bonus is she thinks she can make a real difference in people's lives, while making a difference in her own. This fits right in with her values.

Mike decides the valet job is perfect. Yes, it eats into their Friday and Saturday nights, but the tips are great, and they need to save money and not go out on weekends as much anyhow.

They decide to ask neighbors for help with a garage sale. Although they think Sandy's mom might bequeath them money someday, they decide not to ask her for it now: they want to make sure she has enough for her retirement and don't want her to give them money she might need herself.

They decide to look at a slightly smaller place to live. They don't really need a living room (they hardly use it), so why have one? They don't really need a two-car garage – it's okay if one car stays outside. Besides, they can always look at something bigger again later, and for now, lower mortgage payments will make a big difference. Yes, this will take some explaining to their friends – but true friends will understand that they are doing what they need to do to live better in the long run.

Sandy (reluctantly) decides to give up her weekly manicure visits, with the caveat that she could still go for a special occasion. Mike starts making his own coffee, and buys bagels to bring from home versus buying them at the office.

They decide to go with the credit agency's advice to consolidate their debt as much as possible. And then focus on paying it off as quickly as they can while not incurring new debt.

E = Executed

Sandy and Mike call a real estate agent who helps them find a smaller but very nice home. They consolidate their debt, and cut up high interest credit cards they will no longer use.

Sandy applies to Weight Watchers and gets an interview set up. She knows she'll nail it! Mike takes the job as a valet.

Sandy calls neighbors for their junk. They are so excited someone wants to take it! Sandy organizes a garage sale (with her mom's help) and makes over $900.

Sandy also starts having nail parties at home – a couple of friends come over each week and they do each other's nails. It's actually given her a chance to bond more tightly with some gals while saving money.

Sandy and Mike know it will take years to get rid of their debt and live a financially stable life. But they are on their way.

CHAPTER 11
Frequently Asked Questions About Making a CHOICE

1. **What if you doubt that the choice you are making is the right one?**

When it comes to being CONCLUSIVE, and actually focusing on a path to pursue, we often get nervous. Did I pick the right option? Did I gather enough information? Did I take all the possible consequences into account? What if I'm (gulp) wrong?

Being conclusive on which option to pursue – making "the right choice" - is about making a choice based on the best information available, and with your best guess at consequences. We cannot write the future in pen – circumstances change and we need to adjust, and sometimes the "right choice" has unforeseen consequences. Sometimes those consequences are even better than expected! And sometimes they are not. When they are not, we need to make the best of it by learning and moving on.

2. **Isn't the very fact of being conscious of what choice to make – ala where to change – a choice itself?**

CHOICE's have many choices along the way!

First we choose to improve in a particular area. Then to be hopeful about it. Then we choose to open our minds to possibilities. And then make a choice of what options to put on our list. Next we choose to research and be informed.

Then we choose to think out consequences and then how to come to a conclusion and make a plan of action. And finally we choose to execute against that plan. Every step of the way is a choice within the CHOICE to move forward! And even in every step, there are many choices to be made (for instance, in "Informed" – we need to choose what to research, where to research, how much to research, and even when to stop researching and move on).

3. I've heard of SMART choices. Where do those fit in?

SMART stands for Specific, Measurable, Achievable, Realistic, and Timely, and is often used in goal setting. It comes into play when you are being conclusive in picking your option(s) to pursue.

The more **specific** we can be once we conclude what to do – versus vague in what we plan to do – the more likely that choice will be executed. When we conclude what to do, we also need to make sure it is something we think we can actually **achieve**, and that it is **realistic**. We also want to be **timely** – it doesn't help us to conclude to do something, but then put it off forever. And finally, it is worthwhile to **measure** our results. In the examples in the last chapter – Did Sandy and Mike start reducing their debt? By how much? Did Brian start becoming fitter? He could probably look at his Body Mass Index (BMI), or even the size of his pants, as ways of measuring this. And I bet if you asked Susan to measure how safe she thinks her mom is now versus how safe she was in her old home, the rating would be much higher.

Net, being SMART goes hand in hand with making a better CHOICE.

4. **CHOICE is very linear, but what if you're already in "Execute," and you think of a better option?**

It is perfectly fine to adjust. We often start down one path, and realize another one may be better. But make sure you are doing this for valid reasons, and not just to procrastinate executing against the first option you picked. Otherwise you will be spinning your wheels versus making real progress.

If you are executing, and discover a new option that you think may be far superior, then go back and get information on it to make sure it might truly suit your needs better. If it does, then conclude this will be a better choice, and execute against it versus your original decision of what to do.

5. **CHOICE can take time, and often we don't have a lot of time to make decisions. What then?**

Some decisions we make quickly because they don't have a tremendous impact on our lives. What to order at a restaurant, for instance. But we actually do go through the CHOICE process quickly in our minds. We **consciously** decide to order (we're there to eat, right?), and we may **hope** that we like the food (overcooked would be bad), and we look at **options** on the menu, and we are **informed** about what is in each menu option (i.e.: the hamburger includes a side of fries) and we **conclude** what to order, and then we **execute** by ordering it and eating it.

The more impact a decision has on our life, the more we owe it to ourselves to take the time to go through the CHOICE process more thoroughly to decide what to do. Whether we give it an hour, day, week, month or even longer to go through this process, it is important to do it, as it will make us feel more confident in our decisions as well as make progress against them.

6.   What if I need to make a CHOICE that impacts others, and they don't agree with my decision?

An important part of making a CHOICE is thinking through the consequences. Part of the consequences is how your choice might impact others. If this is a choice that might greatly disturb or negatively impact others, and so they don't agree for that reason, you need to ask yourself if there is a better option to consider that will not cause as much pain or disturbance. Find out why they disagree with your choice. What are the reasons they think the choice is wrong? What consequences do they predict? What alternative options do they recommend? What are the possible consequences of those other options?

And ask yourself – is this a choice that can be made unilaterally, or do you need to use a method to conclude what to do that involves the ones you impact? Instead of "my" decision, does it need to be "our" decision? Often, if it impacts others greatly, it does. Unilateral choices in this case can cause resentment, anger, and a host of other emotions that you do not want.

Let's take an example. Say you absolutely hate your job, and are offered a new opportunity across the country that excites you. But your family doesn't want to move. Your wife doesn't want to look for a new job, your kids don't want to leave their friends, and your extended family wants to keep you closer. You really want this new job – for your own sanity and to build your career. But you are getting resistance on all sides. Don't they understand how much this means to you? Don't they know that this opportunity will let you breathe easier and allow you to enjoy your day (and life) more? Why can't they be more supportive?

It is easy to look at this situation as a "me" versus "them." But it is important to change that into a "we" versus a bad current situation. In this case, the "we" needs to minimally be you and your wife, deciding together on what's right for the whole family, and looking at alternatives that might make you happier while keeping the family relatively happy as well. Are there other opportunities closer to home that might be viable and exciting? Is it possible for you to live away and travel home on weekends until something opens up closer by? Maybe it's time to change careers if you are really unhappy. Is it more acceptable to the family to move within driving distance of friends and family versus across the country so at least the family can see them more often? What is possible? As you talk out options together, open up your minds and explore. The more you do this together, the more likely you'll come up with possible solutions that are more acceptable to all involved.

7. What if I have two equally good options and can't decide between them?

Uh, oh. This is when it really gets tough. Two options that are both great. One is not apparently better than the other – but rather they both have great advantages. Maybe different advantages, but still, really great ones. And neither has vastly horrific disadvantages that eliminate it. So now what?

Well, again first, decide if it really is an either/or decision, or if there is a way to get some of the advantages of both alternatives into perhaps a third one. But if it really is an either/or alternative, and you can only choose one, what's the best way to solve this?

The first thing to do is to ask, "Am I missing something about these options? Do I really know enough about both of them to say they are absolutely on par with each other? If they both have about the same number of pros and cons, are all these pros and cons of equal weight?"

If the information you gathered really doesn't give you enough direction to make a choice between two equally good choices, this may also be the time to bring your instinct into play. To use your gut feeling. What does your heart tell you to do? Your values? Your principles? If you relax and close your eyes, what do you envision when you follow one path versus the other? Does one of these paths look more attractive to you? Why or why not?

In the conclusive chapter, we suggested this exercise: Pick one of the choices. Feel like the other one is off the table. You've made the choice and now you need to live with it. Then take a deep breath and gauge your feelings. How do you feel about the choice? Sense of relief? You probably made the right choice. Sense of anxiety, your gut is telling you that something is off. That this may not be the right choice for you.

Often we will avoid coming to a conclusion because we are afraid of making the wrong choice. So we will say we can't decide because both choices are equally great. Or both choices are equally bad. We are afraid that once we commit, there is no going back, so it is better to just avoid coming to a conclusion. We want to continue to keep doors open so none of them close behind us. We want to avoid the feeling that we are 'losing out' on the other choice.

So ask yourself this question, if you HAD to choose by tomorrow, what would you choose? Give yourself a time constraint to come to a conclusion, and watch how quickly you can. And also tell yourself, I can always adjust. Learn, grow, and adjust. But first, choose.

8. **Don't you have to be informed before you even know what possibilities to pursue?**

Often the open and informed part of the process are iterative - you know some options, you learn about them, and through your learning you hear of other options, and then learn about them. And so on.

It is important, however, to start with an open heart and mind. If we start with "Informed" first, we often close ourselves off to possibilities, *thinking* we know enough. Often we act on assumptions versus true information. "That will be too costly so it's not a possibility." "That's too hard so it's off the table." "My wife would never buy into that, so it's not worth considering." And so on - with many, many reasons why we can't consider possibilities.

So, it's best to reverse this – put the possibilities first. Think of ways that help you change in the direction you want to head – easy ones, hard ones, wacky ones, and sane ones. Then find information that helps you conclude what to do.

9.   **I'm trying to use CHOICE, but I always get stuck on conclusive. It's just too hard to be conclusive! I still don't know what to do. Why am I so indecisive?**

Without knowing what is going inside your brain, there are many things that make us reluctant to be conclusive. We don't want to miss out on something, we don't want to accept that we can't have it all, we don't trust ourselves because some of our decisions made in the past didn't pan out as we expected, we don't want to possibly hurt or disappoint ourselves or others, we don't, we don't, we don't - fill in the blank. Net, a lot of our reluctance to be conclusive is fear based.

Let's look at this with a physical example. Imagine you are walking up to the edge of the diving board, with the deep water below. Will you belly flop? Look foolish to others if your dive isn't perfect? Get too much water in your ears from the impact? There are a lot of reasons we put up walls to keep us on the edge of our diving board. A lot of fears go through our mind about taking the leap and being conclusive.

So here's how to relax a bit more to get over your reluctance. First, realize some decisions don't work out. They just don't. Whether you missed taking something into account or something totally unexpected occurs, it happens to all of us. The greatest achievers often have the greatest failures. So count on failing sometimes. It's okay. We're human. Go into it with an attitude of "This may work, but there's a chance it won't, and if so, I'll learn, adjust and move on."

Second, realize by not being conclusive, you've decided on the status quo. Is that what you really want? If so, fine. Give yourself permission to NOT be conclusive! But if you do want to change the status quo, then consider giving yourself an artificial time limit, maybe even with some great consequences. "If I come to a conclusion on this by XYZ date, I will treat myself to a spa visit."

Third, realize that the past is the past. You don't *have* to repeat bad choices. Even if you are not satisfied with some of the choices you have made in your life, it doesn't mean you will make unsatisfactory choices in the future. In fact, going through this process helps reduce the risk of bad choices.

Fourth, listen to your intuition more. Trust those little voices that tell you something is right or something "just isn't right." Bad conclusions are often made when we go against what our head and heart are telling us to do.

10. Aren't too many options bad? Doesn't that create more stress and make it harder to conclude what to do?

In Psychologist Barry Schwartz's book <u>The Paradox of Choice - Why More Is Less</u>, Schwartz makes a case for reducing the number of possibilities, sharing his analysis of how consumers can get more anxious with too many options.

His work built on studies by Sheena Iyengar, Professor of Business at Columbia Business School, which were published a decade earlier. In them, she showed circumstances in which too many options reduced the likelihood that people will choose any. Ms. Iyengar shared her findings in her book, The Art of Choosing.

While these studies are intriguing, attempts to duplicate these results have had very mixed results. Often studies have shown no meaningful connection between the number of possibilities and stress, or the number of possibilities and the ability to conclude which to pick. In fact, averaged across all studies, the average effect of choice size on our ability to pick, without stress, is....zero.

This doesn't mean that coming to a conclusion in and of itself isn't stressful. We often stress when we conclude because we question ourselves. But what this *does* mean is that it is fine to go ahead and come up with as many options as you can to move you in a specific direction. As you go into the "Informed" stage, you will find that information gathered may support you keeping the option on your list, or support you eliminating it. All this information will then prepare you to move forward to make a conclusion.

11. **I admit I'm a glass half empty person. In fact, I think some cynicism is natural. Why is it so bad to think of what I want to eliminate versus being "hopeful" of what I want to get?**

It is not bad to want to get rid of something that we don't like. In fact, many changes include getting rid of something bad – a job we don't like, a challenging relationship, a health issue, money problems, bullying, etc.

But focusing solely on getting rid of the "bad" doesn't necessarily move us toward the "good." In fact, it can have a counter effect. As we focus on getting rid of the bad, we keep thinking about the bad, and the bad often hangs around longer.

That is why the focus needs to be on what positive result you want, not on what negative result you don't want. Being hopeful means focusing on that positive result. REALLY seeing it as a reality. The more we can train our brains to do this, the better chance we have of moving (and/or moving faster) towards a future that includes the changes we want.

12. I suffer from analysis paralysis. How do I get over this?

Analysis paralysis is, indeed, paralyzing. When we overthink or over research or overanalyze a situation, we avoid deciding what to do. We stay in our "Information gathering" mode, without moving on to a conclusion.

Often analysis paralysis is the result of too much information gathering – we are overwhelmed with what we have put in front of us, and have made the decision overcomplicated. In the search for the 'perfect' solution, we just continue to gather more data. We pile, and pile, and pile it on, until we can't move.

Analysis paralysis is a key procrastination technique. We often use, "I'm still researching" as an excuse to put off a decision because we fear making the wrong decision. As we shared in question 9, it is fear that causes us to avoid being conclusive.

Realize, you can *never* be fully informed, because you can *never* predict the future (unless you're a seer, maybe then, but usually even seers can't see everything). Life is full of best guesses, but there is no such thing as an absolutely perfect decision. Decisions that lead to good results, yes. Decisions that lead to great results, yes. Decisions that lead to unexpectedly bad results, yes. We try our best to make the ones that lead to good or great results, but we are all human. And humans are not infallible. Trying our best means being conclusive and actually *trying* something. Not putting it off and putting it off with analysis, forever analyzing and not concluding how to use the information you've already gathered.

13. Isn't there a different process for business decisions than personal ones?

The process is the same, but the language may be different. In the business world, for instance, terms like "strategic planning" are used, looking at the long term "vision" of the company and determining what strategies and actions are needed to move the company toward that vision.

The company still needs to **consciously** decide what they want to do and be **hopeful** about it. In fact, a lot of their visions will have this hopeful language in it. Let's take Dupont's vision, for example:

Our vision is to be the world's most dynamic science company, creating sustainable solutions that are essential to a better, safer, healthier life for people everywhere.

While we can say that it would be even more powerful if they said "We are..." versus "Our vision is to be..." they have made a conscious decision to be the most dynamic science company, and they are hopeful in their language to do so.

The company then needs to be **open** to the many ways they can pursue this vision. Options are considered in their strategic planning process. Companies often use creativity and brainstorming sessions to come up with possible ways to pursue their vision. The next part of strategic planning includes becoming **informed** about the different options, as well as being **conclusive** as to which ones to pursue and writing these into strategies and action plans needed to move them toward their vision. And then they mobilize their organization to **execute** against these plans.

Companies often have long term visions (10 year is most common, but some do 50 and even 100 year visions!), 1-3 year strategic plans and yearly action plans. There is a scheduled timing to the process. The companies that are most effective review their plans quarterly to see if they are on track or to see what adjustments need to be made. They respond quickly as customer needs change, new technologies develop, new laws are passed, supply issues arise, and other market changes occur that can impact their plans. They review their strategies annually to make adjustments as well.

With all this planning, however, they are basically going through the CHOICE process over and over again. Being conscious and hopeful of what they want, being open to possibilities, becoming informed, then conclusive and finally executing against their plans.

There are a few other differences between a business decision and a personal one. The CHOICE process in business often requires a team in many of the steps. Let's take the conclusion step, for instance. A stakeholder analysis is often done to determine not only who is needed to plan but also who is needed to build ownership and commitment from those that will be responsible for supporting the plan. They need to support the conclusion for it to be executed effectively in the organization. Several decision making techniques for a team (versus just one person making the decision) can also be used as the team comes to a conclusion as to what to do.

But think about it – don't we often have stakeholders in our personal decisions as well? Not all the time – as in business decisions – but our decisions often do involve and impact others, and we often need to take this into account. For example, when parents ask their kids for input on where to go for dinner – they are asking key stakeholders for input. They want to build ownership that the restaurant chosen works for everyone.

Net, business decision-making is not that far off from personal decision making. The biggest differences are the number of people involved and the scheduled timing of the process. But they both go through the CHOICE process.

14. **Where does gap analysis come into account in CHOICE? Aren't you supposed to look at where you want to be, then where you are now, see the gap, and decide how to close it?**

Absolutely!! Gap analysis fits right in with CHOICE. First, we are conscious of where we are now. If this is not where we want to be, then we make a conscious choice to change. We do so because we recognize there is a gap between where we are and where we want to be. So we state where we want to be – this is being hopeful. So now we have where we want to be, and know where we are. The gap. Deciding how to close it takes us into looking at options – which leads us into ways to get from here to there. We then gather information, come to a conclusion and execute to close the gap.

15. **What if what I hope for is really not in my control?**

There are a lot of times when this happens. I know someone who was upset because her teenage daughter just never seemed happy. She set her hope for: "My daughter is happy and thriving." But here is where we need to think about direct and indirect control. With direct control, we have the power to fully make our "hope" happen. With indirect control, we may be able to influence it somewhat, but it is really under someone else's control. This mother can never control her daughter's feelings, but there may be some things she can do to impact them. She can only focus on what she can actionably do to possibly influence those feelings. It is important when we set our hopeful statement to know what we can control and can't control. We can never control the beliefs, feelings, or even behaviors of others. We only have the power to influence them – sometimes greatly and sometimes not that much. We can try to positively impact them, but in the end, it is up to the other person to make changes. In our example, only the daughter can decide when and how to be happy. When the daughter decides to set her own hopeful statement: "I am happy and thriving" and then works on ways to accomplish that, positive sustainable change is more likely to happen.

Likewise, if you set a hopeful statement of "I am CEO of this company," you need to understand that you can only take steps to become it, but it is often up to the company board of directors (and those higher in your corporate ladder along the way) to decide. You have indirect control, but not direct control. With indirect control, we cannot guarantee our hope will come true. But we can continue to work towards it nevertheless.

16. **Can't I just make a decision versus making a CHOICE?**

Yes, of course. We make decisions all the time without consciously going through all of this process. And yet, if we look at most of our decisions, we really do quickly go through these steps in our head. We may not say to ourselves, "Now I am being hopeful." But we often are. We don't say to ourselves, "It is now time to conclude." But we do. Meaning, we may not be used to the acrostic of the word CHOICE – what each letter stands for – but we actually use it all the time. The more you consciously go through the process, making sure to hit every step, the more you will increase your odds of making a better decision. You may not need to do this for decisions that do not impact you that greatly, but for ones that do, it is vital to your success. This book was intended to not only make you more aware of how you make your decisions, but to prepare you to make better ones.

As you finish this book, let me leave you with this final thought:

A fulfilled life is packed with CHOICEs
that lead us to happy moments, days, and years.

Wishing you the best life ever!

Acknowledgements

My heartfelt thanks goes to all those who have influenced me in life, beginning with my mom and dad. They gave me unconditional love and always encouraged me to try my best at whatever I wanted to achieve.

Thank you to my husband, who is my rock and number one supporter. He tells me how wonderful and capable I am on days where I'm not quite sure of myself or when I'm feeling stressed. He makes me coffee every morning and says, "Goodbye gorgeous" before he leaves for work. He is convinced he married the best person in the world, but I know I really did.

More thanks to my children – Jake, Ariella, and Dylan – who have all provided such light in my life. Watching them go after their dreams and mature into caring, successful, and wise adults has been an absolute joyride.

Thank you to all the people whom I have had the pleasure to help in business and in the not-for-profit world. I have gained so much from working with you, and am always so grateful when you share the positive impact that I have had on you as well.

In writing this book, my biggest thank you goes to my contributing author, John Chancellor. I'm not sure I would have taken the time to write it without his encouragement and insistence, his writing contributions, and the ability to bounce ideas off him. I also want to thank all the people who participated in reviewing the first draft, helping to reshape it with a better flow and a steadier tone.

Next in line is my thanks to the amazing Steve Wickham of Wickwood Marketing. Steve is an absolute guru when it comes to knowing the ins and outs of today's publishing world, and he went above and beyond many times in helping me navigate and do what was needed. Steve is not only extremely knowledgeable, but also a great guy - really caring about your success. He is currently developing a program to guide authors from concept all the way to publishing and marketing. If you are writing a book (or even thinking of writing one), I would highly recommend contacting him to learn more about his program and how it might help you. He can be reached at:

www.WickwoodMarketing.com

Thanks also to Jeff Hendler, a great coach who gave me my first interview about the book on his podcast "Bouncing Back." And for all those who have asked to interview me afterwards about it or gave me an opportunity to talk about the concepts at their workplace or to various groups and forums. I have enjoyed working with every single one of you.

Thank you to all the people who researched concepts over the years that were applicable to various points of this book.

Thank you also to Pixelstudio from Fiverr for doing the cover design. You were wonderful.

Finally, a big shout out thanks to all my dear friends and extended family whom all mean so much to me. My life has been a richer experience because you've been part of it.

About the Author

I am happy to admit my life has been filled with great choices. That doesn't mean I've succeeded at everything I've tried – but I view those things that didn't turn out as I hoped they would to be great learning experiences. So nothing is ever a "bad" choice in my mind, as long as I gained new knowledge and understanding about myself or about others along the way.

I have had many fulfilling experiences in my life, both in the business world and on the personal side. In business, I have worked closely with high-level leaders of Fortune 100 companies. Helping them with strategic planning and with making their organizations as well as themselves more effective. I've also worked with a variety of other people in business and in my not-for-profit work. I have lived abroad (in Japan for 3 years) and have traveled the world both for business and pleasure. Throughout my career, I have enjoyed training, facilitating, writing, as well as coaching people and teams to peak performance.

On the personal side, I have been married to a wonderful man for almost thirty years and have three kids who are my pride and joy. I feel blessed every day, and love to foster that feeling in others as well.

To know more about my business consulting and executive coaching, please visit my website:

www.choiceexecutivesolutions.com

or contact me at:

denise@choiceexecutivesolutions.com

I also take a select few private clients who want to work on a personal change outside of the business world.

My focus is to help them *define and accelerate* getting what they want out of life, working with them every step of the way.

If you would like to talk to me about being a private client, please contact me at the email address previously listed.

Also, if you are so inclined, I welcome book reviews on Amazon.com.

To submit a review:

1. Go to **http://Review.PowerOfChoiceBook.com** (This link will take you directly to the write a review page for this book, but you may be asked to sign in.)

2. Answer any of the optional survey questions Amazon may give you, chose the number of stars you would give this book, and add your personal review.

3. Click Submit.

It's as easy as 1, 2, 3! Thanks in advance for your review, it will be helpful to me in many ways and I appreciate you taking a few moments to do it.

Lastly, if you want to contact me regarding how the book has helped you with either a personal or business choice, I love to hear inspiring stories. And you may even get a chance to be featured in an upcoming book I'm considering – giving more examples of how people have changed their lives making great choices. For your story, be sure to include how you went through the six steps to go from being conscious of the change you wanted all the way to how you executed it and got it!

Made in the USA
Middletown, DE
17 December 2016